EROS
OF
ANGELS

A Collection of Poetry and Prose

Radomir Vojtech Luza

authorHOUSE

AuthorHouse™
1663 Liberty Drive
Bloomington, IN 47403
www.authorhouse.com
Phone: 1 (800) 839-8640

Published by AuthorHouse 01/20/2016

ISBN: 978-1-5049-6324-4 (sc)
ISBN: 978-1-5049-6325-1 (e)

Print information available on the last page.

Any people depicted in stock imagery provided by Thinkstock are models,
and such images are being used for illustrative purposes only.
Certain stock imagery © Thinkstock.

This book is printed on acid-free paper.

DEDICATION

To Los Angeles, the city of angels, which has inspired me when I was flat on the ground, loved me when loneliness was my best friend and made me laugh when weeping made me half.

Continue illuminating the universe with sand, surf, sunlight and voices in the library. You mesmerize when you smile. Harmonize while using that incandescent guile. Also, deepest thanks and blessings to Mary Anneeta Mann, Maggie Shumaker and Brian Thorpe without whom this expression of poetry and prose would not have been possible.

And to the love of my life Patricia, who keeps me centered and real.

REFERENCE PAGE

The author also wishes to thank the english language which allowed him
to organize the poetry and prose in this collection alphabetically.

Why? Because english and the alphabet have a certain originality and creative
allure that favor this book, its literary mood and emotional landscape.

--Radomir Vojtech Luza--

Original Art/Sketches by Seth Young

Contents

Part I
Fumbling Towards Family/
Philly To Focus

**Part II
Previewing Purgatory/
Vowels And Verse
From The Streets To Keats**

About The Book

This collection of poetry and prose, then, is influenced by Luza's days of homelessness, hunger, humility and torture wandering the never ending streets of Los Angeles.

Radomir's 26th effort is also chock full of subjects ranging from philosophy to theology, metaphysics to media and love to longing.

But more than any other topic, this collection revolves around the city it was written in: the purgatorial monolith that is Los Angeles. Whether poetry or prose, the City of Angels works its way into almost every nook and cranny of this blessed bible of belonging.

It inspires and elevates this book into a unique glimpse into one man's struggle and ultimate triumph over an unforgiving, brutal and sometimes deadly town. Blood, sweat and tears are spilled in this unholy quest for survival as a young soul in its prime is nearly buried alive underneath the shame, guilt, fear and doubt that endlessly plague it.

In the end, the length of this tome equals the alienation, isolation and resignation that Radomir still feels expressed in syntax, alliteration, clauses and phrases.

It is a significant departure from 2014's "New York Nadir" for Luza in terms of maturity, humility, emotional availability and length.

Here, Radomir proves that perhaps miracles are not only beautiful, but possible, orange yellow not black.

That a city, like Los Angeles, can make you while it is breaking you.

People and places, Luza shows, are not random, but pieces on God's chessboard.

Life, love and time are nothing short of rivers flowing into an ocean of humanity.

"Eros of Angels," then, is that mighty ocean. Its turquoise waters massaging continents and curiosities like a waterfall in Eden.

Eros meaning love. Angels defined as Los Angeles, the City of Angels.

This collection underscores redemption and rebirth that force the reader to look inward into his or her own tortured memories and unfulfilled dreams.

May love come without violence, but with knowledge gained through experience, illumination and education.

And may it come soon.

To Radomir, at least, love is God.

Introduction

There have been many notable poets who luxuriate in the splendor of language and the melodic, intoxicating way it can resonate. There are others who deliberately opt for stark minimalism and the trenchant, jarring affect it can have on us. Some can draw from the turbulence, crisis and injustice that all too often define our world, our statecraft and our headlines. Others may opt for acute introspection, and hope, through some subjective prism, to touch painfully personal chords and make their meaning universally felt.

Then there is Radomir Luza.

We live in an age when all too often the world of contemporary "poetry" is peopled by semiliterate undergrads with bad breath and a six pack hangover claiming to be the next Bukowski or neurotic, misty-eyed "empty-nesters" who read "The Bell Jar" in high school and fancy themselves to be the new Sylvia Plath.

In the midst of this tedium, Luza is a refreshing study in genuine substance and artistry.

Born into a family of distinguished Czechoslovakian artists who suffered the horrors of the nazi onslaught, he has also been cast adrift and alone in the darker regions of the American landscape and is no stranger to the pain and travail of the lost and displaced of our world. Yet, being as resourceful as he is, Luza has transposed the painful trials that might have crippled a lesser man or artist into a majestic array of literary gems that inspire, endear, enchant and entrance with their piercing beauty and heartfelt honesty.

He is that all too rare master of the poet's medium who knows just when and where to utilize all the approaches previously listed without ever sounding forced, synthetic or perfunctory.

Whether celebrating his Lover's eyes in a delicate lyric or detailing with searing accuracy the often brutal grind of life on the urban streets, his words convey a precision that is as achingly precise as it compelling.

One could compare his work to that of Crane or Thomas, Ginsberg or Sandberg, and indeed, at its best, it traverses the same terrain with a skill and sensitivity that certainly ranks him in the same company. In the end, however, he is his own triumphantly independent and distinct visionary who respects the craft and teachings of the time-honored masters without ever sacrificing his own singularly moving and original perspectives.

EROS OF ANGELS, this latest of his collections, combines all of the successes of his previous achievements in a vibrant volume that is at once dramatic and tender, riveting and poignant. Along with a fine assortment of his recent verses, it also gives us a rich sampling of his prose work in which his talents are equally evident. Here again we find Luza as versatile, observant and sentient as ever, taking us from the earthbound to the ethereal, the sensual to the spiritual, the fragile to the formidable.

It may well prove to be his best publication to date and the tantalizing promise of even better works to come.

As one who has had the honor of sharing, reciting, editing and publishing this man's work in the past, I can only hope that this edition reaches an even wider readership than have any of his books so far, and further solidifies his reputation as one of our most gifted poets whose work and example I hope will continue to captivate and endure.

Brian John Thorpe
Poet, playwright and co/editor of The Altadena Poetry Review

Part I

FUMBLING TOWARDS FAMILY/
Philly To Focus

PART 1

TUMBLING TOWARDS FAMILY,
PHILLY TO FOG'S

8TH Avenue

8/16/15

Behind the wand of Fifth and
The bond of Sixth

Are you in your ru suit
Longing for rinse and rhyme
Bag and dime

At 42nd you careen
Into midnight and misery
Like collapsing mule

Gift stores and pocket restaurants
Line ungilded sidewalks
Like unwanted terrorists

Eyes looking you over
Like Filet Mignon
Top to bottom

Plastic cups and open caps of
Dough eyes and trembling wrists begging
For spare change
Dot your spine

Above 48th
3 pm shines through cracks
As buildings glisten and
People listen

Eateries, bars, pubs and bistros
Mark territory
To make you forget
The world's debt

Weeping for darkness
Celebrating light
In middle again
Like heartbroken wren

7/15/15

I am a poet
First and foremost

Putting puzzles on papyrus
People thinking me powerful and proud
Personal and loud

This is my 12th poem in three days
Others would kill for what God gave me

What gift he instilled in me
Talent he retooled me with

Four poems a day
Here to stay
None in the gray

I love writing poetry
Ten hours a day
I pray

I want to start
A publishing company
For emerging poets

Turn American literature around
Let poets be paid
Make poetry a staple in schools

Open the East to Western writing
Like blood through a vein
Ink through a stain

Actress Armed

Trained at the Czech National Dramatic Conservatory at 15
During World War II
My mother never acted outside of her homeland

A talented wasted
An instinct derailed
A wisdom wondering without friends or fairy dust
Dogma denied

America was not for her
Money and fame hardly made her stir

It was the Greeks and Shakespeare
That made her purr
Like a kitten in fur

Catching the eye of a producer or two
She was blue
Of a different hue
Like very few

Crying out "is that it?"
To an actor on the screen
In a crowded movie theatre
She a buzz saw without a name
Acted the game

The brunette haired beauty
Lived in New York City
While the Actors Studio was king
She never auditioned
For fear of masculine sting

My father was frightened of
American bling and
Gave my mother less support than
He should have given that ring

Flying high should have been her blessed thing
But she got caught up in excuses and mental flings
Never allowing herself the chance to sing And spread those big, beautiful wings What was she afraid to bring?

Alone

Do not tell me that I am great
Or bad

Do not free me
Or say you can see me

Hold the door
To your own store

Do not presume to know me
Or owe me

Do not live through me
Or give to me

Let the birds sing
But dare not to my house bring
Jealousy and jail
Fantasy and bail

The days ring
But do not sting

I am myself
I am me

The gray say
What the black and white may

Alone on the Fourth of July

7/4/15

Once more the loneness alights
Without as much as a fight

I sit by myself at the Coffee Bean
On Sunset and Hayworth near the
Sunset Strip again
Sipping a regular coffee
The same one as yesterday

The afternoon getting longer
Nervous legs stay

Harnessed laughter not at bay
Mama and papa watching from above
The son they love

And she goes to her family's dinner
The one I am not invited to
Laughing and singing and talking

I sit at some coffee shop in
Woodland Hills and
Balm my scar

The one never too far
Only to sing myself
Like a meadowlark

I forgive
I redeem myself
But I cannot make a habit of this
It is so far from bliss

Another day
Another soft hiss

Alphabet of Poetry

3/7/15

It means little to me
If odes or sonnets I write

Villanelles and haikus matter not

I care about spilling my truth
The truth of my Czech parents
And grandparents
Who lived under Hitler and Stalin

Who fought with both mind and heart
Ink and bullet

Who are now heroes in their
Homeland after 45 years of war
And occupation

I see this victory of the soul In
the simplest of terms Through
the clearest of vistas Because
simplicity does not Mean
stupidity
Resistance futility

Always Me

Sitting on cutting block
Hit in head by sharpest rock

Neither hinder nor yor
Bullied through those double doors

Yellow skies
Bubble gum lies
Early morning thighs

Begging for snow to stop
Neither flake nor snake

Looking for love
In narrow street

The one elixir
I dare not meet

In darkest city
Falling into retreat

Singing in line
Handcuffed by rhyme
Banging for time

Sun appearing once more
On blessed shore

Like injured whore
With loudest roar
Unafraid to bore

Another Neighborhood Council Meeting

7/13/15

Raised voices
Eye glasses thrown on table
Stances taken
Stances backed off from

Days torn from pages
Pages torn from days

Maybes sworn to like clay
In the emperor's parlor
Amid this fray
Two months after May

I once lived for this mess
Now I wish for less
Masquerading as a guess
On an island with no stress

The highs and lows
Of nine toes
Like a languid lion
I suppose

Make me think
Of you and me and
How we differ from this
Abhorrent glee

How we stare at the bee
In its hive
Yes where it is free

Radomir Vojtech Luza

Ash Gash

8/25/15

Under rotund sky
Planes fly

After 9 a.m. Twins die

First one
Then the other

Like tall brother
Of same mother

Each and every one of us
Draining puss

Dust on eyelashes
Glass under silk sashes

Stories told forever
Blood in Hudson River

Like caged bird
Life absurd

Fall in love
Like alabaster dove

Tell and warn
Sell and mourn

Give and live
Stop the sieve

Like native New Yorker
Giving birth
On green earth

As the Train Passes Me By

8/22/14

Death is a black hole
Made of love

Life lingers like a lost
Thunderstorm

And the sins and sinners
Bylaws and bellies
Arguments and angels
Pass me by

Riptides ricochet against
Ribald rocks

Animals angle awkward
Arias against anger

As the train passes me by
The difference between me and
You evaporates

Leaving behind a vapor of
Candy and corn
Like pierced potatoes
Populating Peoria

Divine names are given to the few
Divinity has no friends
And as many problems as
The front page has tragic headlines

I have seen the ugly and the good and choose the good
Without thought or hesitation
Like an exuberant monk singing at dawn
Sinking strong and digging deep

Easy is climbing the devastation without a rope
Hard to cope
As the train passes me by

Radomir Vojtech Luza

At the Coffee Bean Again

The air is thick with tennis shoes
And a trembling muse

The poetry comes and goes
Like peppermint fuse

In between I dine on emptiness
And lower dues

On Sunset near Fairfax
The hungry have no name
And the well to do all the game

There is no music here
Merely the beating of drums
With no rhythm

The cascading of thumbs
Without a hand

The banging of tom toms
With no band

The gap between rich and poor
Maybe the largest in the land

Glares riding travails
God details

In West Hollywood tonight
Lights shine

Tank blazes
Cardinal crows
Pastor runs to the rectory

Musicians the stage
Comedian his rage

I sit at the Coffee Bean inhaling fumes
I should have put out long ago

At the McDonalds
on Riverside and Lankershim

Mo, the 93-year-old
With the loud mouth
Is threatening
To hit somebody with a pipe

At this hamburger joint
This grilled cow cacophony
That is not unusual

Nomads
Directionless and misled
Find a home here

Amid employees and managers
Wondering why they do not just get a job

If it were only that easy
If the ifs and whys added up to
Some hows, whens and wheres

If my todays multiplied
Into ten tomorrows

If Mo did not have to holler because
His trembling fingers belie a tortured young boy

His eyes like bruised jellyfish
An insecure countenance
Sockets sucked solid

I do not approach you
Mo for a little like you I may be
Not yet ready to see

Atlanta

Peachtree
Populating my present
Like dancers do discos

Hated first job out of college
Loved the people,
Well, most of them

Getting fired was a holiday

Even public relations firms
I would never return to
They dehumanize and divide

Now actor and writer
I fall in love with Midtown,
Downtown, Buckhead and Dunwoody

Youth sprawling before me like buffalo
Open eyes see
Unblocked ears hear

Friends keeping me tethered to
This world like anchor

Life beams once more
Art a bridge to sanity

Actor not who I am
Writer in subconscious
Words in blood

Hotlanta you saved me by throwing me against brick wall
Only to strengthen the armor

Daddy your eyes like big planets
In small universe

Baby

2/28/15

I want a baby
But my fiancé cannot have one

I want a child
But I must adopt

I want a child
But my wallet is locked

I want a child
But I am a child myself

I want a child
But there is not enough time

I want a child
But inspiration is waning

I want a child
But God's translation is baning

I want a child
But, well, I'd rather write

Backfire

Sitting at the Starbucks on Camarillo and Tujunga
In North Hollywood
You seem like a gentle, old soul

Little did I know
Of the gallows that silenced
Your scream

The combat that
Soiled your sin

The very target on your back
Stemming from a life of lack
On this planet of reverse attack

Blaming me for suicidal thoughts
Is like taking aim at the
Weather man for rain

Or the teacher for
A failing grade

You have taught me to be
Economical with my advice

Careful who I Give tutelage to

So I do not make the bad worse
Turn Ford into hearse

Balance Beam

6/25/15

Aghast at this older man
Making suggestions about my life

Olive shirt
Crow pants

Do not water my brain plants
Like soul ants

A balance is not present
He says

In the second floor office
With couch and two chairs

A game plan is missing
Walking and green salads
Silence the hissing

The door swinging wide
Like the chain on my side

Next appointment is set
A pair in waiting room sit

Balance that remains
Like grass that stains

He the doctor in Hanes
Me the stallion that gains

Balancing Buddha

Under the wings
Of yesterday's memories
Words bounce and boil

Tongues wag and wound and
Genius is left outside
Standing in the rain
Like stranded cattle

The rainbow of ribald roustabouts
Peaks in the sun
Under dreams lost and won
Audiences found at the point of a gun

Never solid or sane
Lonely just for game
On this shore of unheralded bane
We share the same name
Looking and laughing
Like some dame

Brilliance sits alone
While mediocrity finds a home
Like some candle not blown
On this gathering storm of
Muddle and moan

Lost to flashes of a groan
Like dust to a bone

Unwanted and unknown
Perched beneath a throne

Bark in the Dark

This chimney without reason
Cause of the season
Michel angelo of the hour
Roar with no power

Has me by the tail and
Will not let go

This occasion by liaison
Has no tomorrow or yesterday
Only a bitter ending
As in a play

She holds the cards and
I like some shaman at midnight
Wander blessed avenues
Alive with black
Toiling in tan

Like me
Not knowing
Forever from always
Never from bald days

Barriers Brandished

8/22/14

To feel is to live
To die is to isolate

To think is to churn ice cream
To sleep is to let go

Banging on winter's door
Are ice and snow

White as cocaine
Transparent as the death of God
In this unforgiving town
This stalwart stanchion of
Brotherhood and banishment

Buying and selling the clouds
Like alabaster doves

Sealing and dealing lives lost in anticipation

Roses rot
Carnations crumble
Murderers mumble

Hands tremble
Skin pales
Wrists wrangle wrinkles

The reason for existence far outweighs that against it

Bartering by the Beach

Baritone barkeep
Bleeding berated banshee

In this town of brick and back
Losing battle behind an ounce of smack

The police buy hell
By painting purgatory
In yellow and black

Homeless shelter
Sun swelter

Maybe we can lay down
The helter skelter

Like pigeons on a wire
Or bullets on fire

Like the kind of finger
That triggers a linger

Between dust and Darwin
Dreams and dishes

Love in the twilight
Bending in the dark

Like frozen corpses
Unwilling to lend a spark

Base to Camp

The air up here is perfect for love

Perfect for the kind of genocide only bees know

The tattering tottering vowels that turn suffering into sacrifice

And fire into burnished steel

The valleys and hillsides of my dreams carry grenades in their arms

And sub-machine guns in their dreams

Bludgeon me with blueberry rain

And enough sabres for a spiritual awakening

Dawn has come too early but the night was too long

Tell me once if you have not a million times why I should be glad to be alive

And I taste the sweet nectar of the coming hours rife with victory and vowels

Basic Training

7/14/15

By the river I sit
Having another fit
Like an infield hit
Not finding a mitt

Water cooling my feet
Jesus tending to the heat

It is you I greet
My friend
My companion obsolete

On this island of no defeat

Once I open my eyes
I see the flies and
Hear the cries

Of unsung sighs and
Unused thighs

In this palace of lies and
Unforgiven highs

Please friend
Do not bend
Or for flowers send

Merely be
On this concourse of three
Me, you and he

Be

Lock it up and feel it
Smack it don't steal it

When the Beatles rejoiced in it
How right they were

I can repeat it
But not unbead it

To see and not flee
Lend but not bend

For if I let it be
I am a flea
On the way to
The bubble gum sea

I do not care what they think
Or do
Or leave in the stew

It is me versus me
Replacing anxiousness
With consciousness
That good or bad
Lends itself to a lifetime
Of restlessness

Beauty in Everything

7/10/15

The days of darkness
Hours of ardour
Escape me

I see the beautiful
For I am ready
I step down not

The forests The
midnights The
flying kites

Amy Winehouse has come and gone
Sylvia Plath gassed her gullet
William Inge ended a superior life at 61

But I am still here
Weeping at falling stars
Laughing at nothing at all

Jumping out of the sofa
When Serena Williams wins
Another Grand Slam

I see beauty in everything
Because it sees me
Embracing joy

I go against every fibre of my
Bipolar makeup and
Scream in fits of ecstasy

Yes Virginia
There is a Santa Claus
And a God

Bedroom Ears

12/8/14

The love that once rolled like dice
Now cold as South Dakota in January

Strong is not strong enough
Not anymore

Fists pump like forgotten lovers
Tears roll down cardboard cheeks

Hands tremble like evicted tenants

The difference between sanity and insanity
An orange butterfly either way

Today has not been a good day
The bad outweighing any golden bray
The winds whirling around my skull
Like forgotten cheetahs

Inspiration lacking any
Semblance of regard

Inside my stomach twirling
Like Wallenda falling from rope

Love rippling its way across this fertile face

I left you today for a slice of May
Neither black nor white
But giddy gray

Bee of the Sea

7/15/15

Tighter than my size 14 Nike tennis shoes
Wider than the reason for logic

He talks to listen to his own voice
His truth is his own

I believe what I feel
What I know
Not so much anymore
What I see

Oh one above
Guide me through the trees
The unruly seas

July has been difficult
A bee in my bachelor's degree

I hope I can make it through
This ungodly stew
Like a chef with a good review

Truth lies in the good done for others
The love shown by
The few to the many

If that is love
I am an alabaster dove
Flying above

Like being still
On the back of a dollar bill

Radomir Vojtech Luza

Beelzebub's Bargain

The skinned skeleton
Of my soul

Marches over the causeway
Like a stilted scarecrow

The refrains of midnight wakes and
Early morning jazz funerals

This French Quarter
Faubourg Marigny of stolid tears
Looking for solace from name
Sobriety from shame

While the world watches
The pall stretches

I do not belong
Where the river
Meets the song

Where the wrong and strong
Converge in a hailstorm of light and sight

Please papa bludgeon me not with words

Stab me with that stare or
Rape me with that ego

Beelzebub's Hand

Half the time I don't know
Whether to weep or run
Leave or stay

The other half
I hope I am
In the right frame of mind

If the artist in me
Does not devour the producer

Or the lead singer the poet

The comedian the politician
All the time I wonder
Whether this fear of fame is
Keeping me from it

If money and dreams
Do not underscore style over substance
Trembling knees over stalwart thighs

Devil's shaking wrist
Over God's sturdy shoulders

If they turn me into someone
My mirror does not recognize
My ego devours
Because I am so small

If this town is not a subway stop
On this journey of life
The very bus bench of my connection

Beneath the Pool

Finding the light
Beneath the pool
Without a school

Like ordering breakfast with no rule
From my friend Abdul

Please let music change this world
As much as any politician can

Moving pictures
And live performance ran
From the dragon like a man

Abandoning the harshest fool
Must be our best tool

Sitting on a mule
To find the path beneath the pool
Where tomahawks and teepees once ruled

But now
Death and meth stink like bloodied stool

Best Friend

2/26/15

Eyes open like garages
Yesterday's wounds matter not

We ride into Beelzebub's bakery together
Slowly slinging rice

Between your rough hands
And my soft middle I am
Weeping like the boy in the fountain

If love is hell
I am in darkest dungeon
Begging for golden gargoyles
To lift me to softest sand

Please dearest friend
Park the ambulance by the manipulated meadow

I will always love you like a lighthouse hugs the shore
And my dearest father the brightest bookstore

Better Times

6/17/15

Scaling the bars and walls of
The prison cell

The past sleeps
With the present

In a bed of feathers
Plucked from souls
Without appropriate measures

I seek transparent hearts
Like great white sharks

Fins moving like sins
In the maelstrom of the day

Grins giving birth to wins

The malady of death
A cacophony of meth

Mired in this land of Seth
Like fallen pins

Daydreams populate like twins
With this sweeter gin
Caressing bin like so much fallen tin

Between Orange and Yellow

8/22/14

Mockingbird kisses the sun
Pine tree finds the latest pun

Living alone today
I pull the razor near the vein

Passing buildings and alleys
Thunderbolts and homeless valleys

The spirit touches me
Like a baby's laughter

Everest and K2 matter not
I climb my hill of misery
My mountain of molestation

Maybe love can rescue us all
Maybe we will find compassion
When the rock bleeds

Between orange and yellow
Hovers the moon
Like incinerated carp
Lying in wait

Between you and me
Lies an ocean of misunderstanding
Orange and yellow
Like sunshine
Opening bridges for wayward souls and
Misbegotten lies

Billiard Balls

People are watching me
Like broken billiard balls

Looking at me like the
Difference between breakfast and binging

Observing me like Hitler's shadow
Or Stalin's stain
Fully and totally

Few make it through unscathed
None scott free

Most are souls in a box or
Hearts in a cage

Singing in the shower
But never on stage

Writing in journals and diaries
But never published

Giving up is easy
Staying the path is difficult

Then there is love
Which many want
But few know how to get

All need but some devour

People are staring at me
But I don't scare easy

I stare back and unfurl my flag

Blowing Blues

When does giving end? Taking begin?

The bible sits in the corner
Like an abandoned lover

I stand under the light
Waiting for misbegotten moments and
Wavering wanderers

The wrinkles grow more obvious
The scars more true

On bad days I wish for tears
On good ones more King Lears

Sleeping above the equator
Daydreams burn like pungent sun
Trombones blow like tangent gun

Blue Bacon

On days that come
Like giants without a scream

I look to you to swallow my dream
Without a seam

The nephews and cousins of
Comedy are few

They mingle and move
Till night is light and Kite is in flight

I often hear the silent banter
From those on stage
Who cannot lean
Only to a rigid extreme

I dare not applaud
For they aim for laughter
At any cost

If yesterday were tomorrow
Buddha, Jesus and
Allah steam

Perhaps then would these
Hipsters of the dark
Find breath enough to even talk

Blunt Backhand

3/13/15

The backwards groan
Ripped the dead from their slumber

The living from the orange yellow number

I write without drugs or alcohol or cigarettes

Relying solely on gut and confidence
Love and loneliness

In that angled square
I find all I need

I see the new
Discard the glue
Embrace the blue

Nothing you can show me
Will change me

Everything you bring my way
Has already gone through this bay
On some other day

Boca Raton

I have never been to Boca Raton
But I would like to go

Maybe I will end up there
When I retire

When the reasons that I have to go
Outweigh those that I do not

When the love I have for myself
Is strong enough to bring me to you
Boca Raton

When all the critical, suicidal and dark thoughts add up to
A move that does not change the world
But me as a human being

When all the fame and awards and riches mean
A hill of H20

I come to you Boca Raton
For you are the future glued to the past

I wish for one moment
That I was not me
But you Boca Raton

For then free and easy I would be

No social hang-ups or artistic compromises
Would my shoulders bear

But love and light
Like a pair of halogen headlights

Bosom Breath

7/28/15

By the beach
By the beach
Air is within reach
The divine breach
Stinks to highest purgatory
Like some bird sanctuary

Jesus and Satin on the run
A mother's pun
Father's gun

Demonstrations down the alley
Building in the valley

Stay or go
I do not know
So I do nothing

Maybe the blow
Will be slow and
The band at hand
Will leave no production grand

While I wait
For bait
In a world that
Is not late

In deciding my fate
On this very date
Holding my mate

Box

Jack must have forgotten Jill
On the hill Sunday
Around 8 p.m. in Hollywood

His store on Sunset and Cahuenga
Was not mine

It was not fine
This insane asylum where
I chose to dine

One man hardly stood
Another ran up and down the order area
With an empty plastic cup

When I was once homeless
This was a great restaurant

Where tinsel town's good, bad and ugly
Showed up

Today it was only the bad and the ugly

Once the three police cars got there
Half the store emptied

Across the street at Amoeba Music
Three people were arrested

When I ordered the two
Breakfast sandwiches using coupons
I was happy

As I left
My smile had turned upside down

Next time
I will pack some worldly knack
Into my hamburger sack

This Jack
Had a definite lack

Boy and Girl

One likes trees
The other bees

Boy finds knees
Scraped in fleas

Girl sips tea
In open sea

I fly to the edge
Like an iron wedge

Standing near a hedge
On a flimsy ledge

I weep tears that wane
She comprehends the right brain
Like a flower in the rain

Please see through the pain
So I may find the grain

Before I go insane

Breaking the Rules (Not the Laws)

Writing in rainbows
Clearing causes with no clauses

Poetry like hurricane
Battering bridge between bones
Verse never obtuse

Leaping like laryngitis
Over clichés

Tackling soft eyes
Like linebacker beaten thighs

Pen spilling pink sun
Over bengal moon

Rebels with ink
Protest on paper

Supple soaring
Bet without net

Mother would be scared
Father die

I fly like hummingbird with blue sky
Lips with no lie
Tomahawk without sigh

Bucks of Star

The dark roast stains my teeth
Like a Shakespearean sonnet
Or a high speed train with
No respect for ripe meadows or green pastures

The Valencia orange refresher
Tastes like a soft drink
And wakes you up like a
Kurasawa film

The espresso is as strong
As my mother's talent
And as short as my father's temper

The Fizzio soda is as sweet
As my fiancée can be
And as sugary as a road trip to
The past once was

The Frappuccino lasts as long as a Joe Namath pass
And is as intense as a Johnny Cash song

This Starbucks
This bucks in my star
Opens capillaries
And closes bloody veins

It dares me to roll the dice on me
And never loses

It is a marathon and a sprint
A gargoyle and a gift
America and Amanda
Darwin and David

Burying Bad Blood

7/18/15

There is bad blood
Between you and me
So much I'd like
To free

Even more I would decree
Forgotten and forgiven

Or do we both need it
To get us through 3 am
To validate some disagreeable right
On another anxious night

Life is hard
Even with the bard

This makes it darker and danker

If truth be told
This rancor
Makes our touch colder and
Numbness that much bolder

It is anything but gold
To sit in this fold
Because of some purpose foretold

If misery loves company
We are both alike
At least in the manner in which
We bitch, itch and stitch
Like artists yearning
Our least to ditch
In an impossible pitch

Busy Typing

3/11/15

My fiancé wants to love me
I am busy typing

The sun is burning
I am busy typing

The lepers are dying
I am busy typing

My heart is fracturing
I am busy typing

My aspirations call for me in my sleep
I am busy typing

My cousin wants to show me the moon
I am busy typing

My soul requires massaging
I am busy typing

My instincts are ripped from my gut
I am busy typing

By and By

The underbelly of the city shines tonight
Like a scuffed penny

I have much to learn
A poetic style to develop
A vocabulary to expand

The ceiling is whipped cream white
The basement banana black

In between I lie
On my new Serta Perfect Sleeper
Murdering sleep like it was an unwanted child

Putting together poems in my head
Like robust rabbits
Like the difference between oxygen and anger

One laptop white
The other crimson brown
Assembling lyrics I will not sing
On stages I will never grace

My final golden rap
My very victory lap

Eyes dark with potent skies
Ears quiet with church bells

By and Bye

God erupts from the bible
Like a lover of man
God is love

No big bang
Monkeys with fangs

No atoms colliding
Like trains

Just Jesus and me
Holding hands
Hugging strands
Never letting go

God is my shepherd I
shall not want
Evolution wrong font

Darwin have a beer
Do not sneer
Seven days make my world
Without a fear

Adam and Eve in the garden
They are already here

California East

8/23/15

The garbage truck growls down
7th Avenue near Times Square
At 5:32 a.m.

Sanitation workers dispose of
Road side trash as if
It was a Jujubee

Another day
Another late summer sunray
Another light gray May

Sizzling and hissing in the
Mid morning sun

We lumber like grizzlies at midnight
Looking no searching for
Nearest coffee shop,
Juice bar or yogurt shop

Where tapping fingers
Meet busy feet

Take away sky scrapers and freeways and
The two coasts meet in the middle

Like Milwaukee on steroids or
Minneapolis in mini skirt

Screening at Director's Guild on Sunset Boulevard
Ends early

Q and A afterwards
Audience in hushed tones and
Plaid t-shirts
Glass doors bouncing off tanned thumbs

Directors of
Pink pom poms and
Late nights jaunts

Laughing at life
Weeping at strife
Carrying a plastic knife

Cartoon Head

7/11/15

Tell Iron Man about Hercules
Let the Hulk know about Zeus

Inform Captain America
About King Creon

Send Aqua Man a message
About Aquarius

Let Marvel know
That it is not so

The Greeks came before
The Romans a little after

A bedrock of humanity
Is in jeopardy

Why comic book characters?
More surface than game
More superficial than name

The obsession without confession
Lingering doubt with no clout

Shakespeare, Shaw and Shepard
Hemingway, Fitzgerald and Thoreau

Characters not cartoons
Souls not tolls
Parthenon not al-anon

Caterwauling Canary

Counting clicks
In a pond of licks

Like dead end dicks
A Vegas fix

Juice runs down my leg
Like metal peg

With borrowed keg
I beg

Life always better
Than stillness
In the shadows of
My Lochness

Red forgot
White and blue

On this geometric island
Of steep decline

Tunnels are dusk
Treaties musk

And the difference
Between us and them
God as a husk
Southern busk

Central Park

In the middle of Central Park
I sat with my best friend Larry James

Speaking into a recorded microphone
I waxed metaphysical
Waned philosophical

Love was against me
Time was not for me
The city shot me

But Central Park
Green and blue
Purple and new
Was for me

Central Park
In its broken azaleas
And burned out bathrooms
Took me in for one long afternoon

But you Central Park
That burns and breaks
Builds and bakes
Barbequed my yes to my no
And made me swallow below

Child, oh, Child

Sometimes the world stops
The music ends

Often the day dawns string bean green
And dusks beet red

Child, oh, child
Heed the call
Child, oh, child
Do not betray the fall
Steer your way clear of the brawl
Never consider yourself too tall

Many speak of the dark side
Few of the light

Child, oh, child
The sky sees your flight
The falcon soars
The eagle roars

But today you fix the levees that silence your door
Child, oh, child
Ask not for more
The angels have opened a store

There you learn how to pour
With these fingers you never tore

Child, oh, child
Learn how to lead
For we beg for a way out of the greed

Mount that mighty steed
So we may all learn how to need

Christian Counselor

Breeze coming through window
Interprets bible

In stray sleeves
Uncommon patterns

Pounding good book
Like forgotten relic
Lost in must

You enter car wash
Headlights on
More like them than him

Homosexuals extraterrestrials
Dead end
Power does not mend

Brow furrows
Voice burrows
Love a sparrow

Counselor man losing battle
Like Ozzie and Harriett
Gilligan and his Professor

You must go down to go up

Christmas at Denny's

12/25/14

At 51 Christmas is as clear as
The chicken noodle soup I rarely order
It cuts like a rusted knife

My lady love eats Christmas dinner with her family

I order the holiday turkey and
Dressing dinner at the Denny's nearby

Maybe I will not have a family again
Maybe I will continue to spend Christmas dinner by myself

Writing and thinking and looking out the window

Maybe the difference between
The way things are and the
Way we want them to be
Is a little bit of healing either way

This hurts
This bites and fights like a snapping turtle

People can be as cruel as
The weather
And not know it

They can ruin lives with a single word
And pretend not to notice

They can upend empires and destroy lives
And hardly blink

They can be oceans that eat small streams or
Rivers that consume creeks

But right now
I feel like a small stone
At the bottom of the sea

Circle

I know not why hours and days pass me by
Like a pregnant blur

Like the very reason I talk to strangers
And hug homeless people

Because love expressed is almost always
Better than love repressed

This fairytale of a life shattering
Into pieces before me
When hugs are not returned
Embraces not embalmed

The pressure I put on myself
Topped only by that of society

I hear you mother speaking to me through
Flabbergasted ear drums and caterwauling eyeballs

A thousand miles away another slumbers
And I die a million deaths
Waking to dreams of her rumbling through
My subconscious
Like a freight train off the tracks

Minutes and seconds whipping by me
Like so much solar garbage

Cleveland Part II

Answers are questions
People as warm as hot tea

Rock N' Roll showcase
Suburban and sexy

I was the last person out
Music documented like dominos

Downtown dark and
Debonair like Clark Kent

Newspapers rich and
Well written like Frost poetry

Cavaliers close to the
Champagne if three are better
Than one on defense

Meet me in the dog pound
Where Johnny Manziel plays like a rookie

Indians in the hunt every September

I am in Canton with the
Pro football busts
Last person to leave again

Eagle spreading its wings
You are the city by the city

Cleveland
You open my sweet soul
Like no other town

Bless my hands with forgiveness from above

Maybe one day with adopted child

Like caterpillar
Blossoming into butterfly

Coffee Bean
Downtown LA

The crippled boy in his early 20s
Asking people for money
As he drags his legs across 7th near Flower

The African-American man
Right leg the size of two
Inching along 6th near the FedEx

The Oriental girl behind the counter here
Wondering why
The Ferguson protesters
Don't have jobs

But if they did
Some good old fashioned peaceful protesting
Would take a bruising
A battle worth losing

And what I see out of these
Five panes of windows
I do not want to see again
Do not wish to take home with me

It hurts too much
Scars the skull

Who are we?
Where are we going?
Or was my mother right?
This is purgatory

Large black man in t-shirt, torn jeans and bare feet
Talking to himself next to garbage can on 7th

I am safe but for how long?
Do I wish to be protected?
From myself perhaps

Human beings are not enclaves from
But windows to the soul

Coffee on the Corner

I drink it black
Like midnight

The traffic passing before me
On this Saturday night
On Sunset Boulevard

Calming the scarred nerves
The parched soul

The difference between where I am
And where I want to be
As thin as a potato chip

Our national relics tainted
By misunderstanding and morbidity

Our best minds colored
By tan rainbows
And 2 a.m. dawns

Jumping from bridges
Too narrow to consider
Too wide to ignore

Coffee Shop Blues

12/4/14

Here at Gloria's
In the Burbank mall
The tables are as round as sin
As unsteady as love can be

You learn to go for what you want
The bulls eye
Gold medal of lifetimes

Giving is equal to taking
Fame and wealth are monsters that taste like Filet Mignon
And addiction can be as good as it is bad

Where therapy can be a spring board
Not a setback
And the difference between failure and success
Is a few laps either way

Here at Gloria's time is Veronica
Standing behind the counter without a nametag
Waiting to break free from herself

It is the lady across from me
Eating a pastry, it seems, to get away from
The pain of a life stuck in reverse

And me in my brand new Sears jacket and black hat
Searching for the elusive truth again and again

It is me observing woman after woman
And making up my mind
To stop looking at them as objects
And putting them on pedestals
As difficult as that is

Me being true to my fiancé
And knowing that if I spent
One intimate moment with another woman
It would murder her heart and kill our relationship
For she is a tender and fragile soul
It is time ripped apart like fresh tomato
Existence massacred like dead Grizzly

Here at Gloria's
You learn to accept what you cannot stop
Stop what you cannot accept

Cold

Mid afternoon misgivings
Give way to late evening tragedies
In this cauldron of cacophony
This unmitigated attempt at arrogance and irony

Please do not leave me in the cold
Do not spin that merry wheel of
Corpulence and greed

That unerring litigator of
Antonyms and artistry lost
In this maze of unchivalrous
Knights and star laden eves

Please do not leave me in the cold
Take me to where gingerbread men
Frolic in the sand
Like diamonds in the sun
Or letters in the alphabet salsa
The frozen tundra of your soul

Take me under your arms
Where forests grow
And melodies catch fire
Like snow after a blizzard

All I know is that it has taken me
Time to cross this border
This willowy collection of branches
And possibilities tarnished by the early morning glare
Of your belated moon light

And I will not be left in the cold again
Will not fight that most noble of fights with eyes closed

Combustible

The golden wheat hair of you
Is branded by bordellos too small
To see and too thick to steal

You and the life you call a
Success drip in victim's spit
And hypocrite's tongue

I would like to love just once
And not have to be sorry I did

Not have to follow your teeth
Down that misbegotten boulevard of tears

Or my lips through the
Draconian forest of fear

I want confidence
In myself and those around me
Like a puppeteer his puppets
Voter his elected candidate

The ice thaws at dusk
Water runs into a stream
Like rivers into oceans

Blue jays bite the mid afternoon air with song

Computer

I fear making mistakes
On your controls and keys

Where will it lead?
How much material will I lose?
How much time will it take me?

Imbalance stemming from paranoia and paucity
Bad moments ahead
Fears unrealized

Sweetest computer
Working on you keeps me sane

Happier I was before
You came along

No fear of future
Or life ahead

Corner

On the corner of Fairfax and Sunset
The hookers come outside to
Ride the rainbows
And steal the roller coasters

Like fairy dust
They sprinkle sex on the
Cement sidewalks of Hollywood

Kissing carnivals they never knew and
Tolerating the needle infested arms of
The Russian dolls
And Ukrainian divas
These walls protect

On the corner of Sunset and Fairfax
I find unicorns wrapped in Rolex
Riding red

I want to know their names
But maybe they do not have to tell me

Crawling into Bed

3/13/15

Your thin arms hold me
Like a dying skeleton
On the day after Halloween

The face you hide from the sun
Shines in the dark
Like onyx burning

You do not want me to go
I do not want to go
But I do

Leaping into two am
Like a lubricated lion
A lost lavender
Looking for least
In the face of asteroid angels

And the kind of diary
Even thin arms cannot know

Czechoslovakia

Communist boots marching
On Czech homeland
Like black spikes on ripe meadow

Grandmother on mother's side
Slit her wrists in tub

40 years of walls and empty halls
Aunt cleaning blood
Like martyr on call
Waiting for latest fall

No time for revenge or tears

I move on seeing the sun rise
Samurai who cries

Eagle soaring over pistols and pastures

I know I have never seen my mother numb

Daddy put the Typewriter Down

3/7/15

Every morning, afternoon and evening I heard you typing in the study

As a third grader I wondered why you were spending
More time with the typewriter than me

I resented you.

Now, nearly 45 years later, I realize the magnitude of your struggle

Daddy, your Czech accent haunts me like a determined dagger
The iron voice a certain stagger

You lived like you drove a car
Focused and fair
Courageous and bare

Leaving behind career, country and cause for
Caterwauling crow

Daddy, your trembling hands
Belie a strength sautéed in
Prague Spring and sand
Love and land

The seven books I have not read
I will before I am dead

I thank you for the words said
They stay with me like buried lead

Dance Floor

11/23/14

Down at Fads Night Club outside New Orleans
In the Summer of 1983

My best friend Patrick Moreno and I
Discoed, boogied and bee bopped
Our childhoods away

We both wanted something more
Than high school and college

We found it there amid the
Lights, confetti and fog that
I can still smell to this day

Amid Michael Jackson, Irene
Cara and Billy Idol we owned the joint

The alcohol flowed
The slow dances turned fast
And the small problems and issues
Of our lives disappeared
Like leaves in the wind

Patrick and I bonded like brothers
Often wearing the same punk garb
To impress the ladies
But never betraying the truth of the moment
We were looking for love like squirrels do nuts
Absolute beginners do gold

Dark Skies

7/18/15

The means justify the ends
Some people think

Others disagree
Many do not think at all

Love is the answer
The Beatles say and
Millions more agree

Leading us to the golden sea
Without a degree
Like a child climbing a tree

Nothing is free
Fighting for love
Is not glee
But it is me
Active like a worker bee

Toxic is he or she who is not we

Those who stray
Pay a fee

They seem to decree

The key is sipping tea
While taking a knee
At midnight times three

Day After

12/8/14

The day after has
The heart of a skinned skunk
The skin of me and you
The very ambiance of poetry stew

It harks and heralds
To the sky

It never asks if it already knows
It does not know if it asks

The day after hastens and
Harasses the moon
Like a furious lima bean does salt

It hangs its head
Like a praying mantis
And laughs not
For gentlemen die their own deaths
Like severed cows

It maneuvers and manipulates the water
Like centipede on church bell

The day after listens to
Bellowing of bandannas
Blue of Santa Anas

The swan like manna on this island
Of wranglers and rancid wrens

December

Mother in midnight black dress
Moving like love struck mime
Around Christmas tree

Sister and I waiting in bedroom for Jesus
Not Santa Claus
To deliver gifts in the living room
Of our little brick house
On Calhoun Street
In uptown New Orleans

We ask mother to wait with us
She says she has dishes to wash
And tables to clean

We do not believe her
But play along because we love her

Grilled fish, potato salad, turkey and cranberries
Followed by Austrian sacher torte

I have dreamed of this for a year
Mother serves us like dancing sprite in the kitchen
I hold hands with her and embrace the brisk Southern night
Like a leprechaun green grass
We speak Czech
Which no one at Holy Name of Jesus, my grammar school, understands

And I used to think made me an outsider

December you fickle breeze
Finding me joyous and jingle free

Open your skin
Close the door on my sins
Like my father always slams
The door to make a point

Rid the Middle East of its satin Satin
Subtract the evil I have done
From the good and let it equal some love

Some red blooded American tolerance
The kind that opens closed minds

And travels the Sahara without a camel

I sing in the rain December
Like a forlorn fawn lost in the forest

After the presents are opened
We stay up until three or four in the morning
Playing air hockey, electric football, and Battleship

Mother making a list of gifts to return and give me next year
Me dreaming of more G.I. Joe and Big Jim accessories

Jesus massaging his lower back from all the heavy lifting

Sweet December
Seventeen days earlier
This bomb baby celebrates his day of birth
And a week later a new 365 commence

Your 31 waste not want not
Sparkle not spoil

Detour at Dawn

3/13/15

In the mingling and mining
Of minds
The strawberry sins graduate first

The granola bar of agony
Lurches and lands
On the ribald island of
Misfit midgets

We swim and saw
In the waters of love
Only to find a boulevard closed
Or a street ripped to its core

At dusk the divine flow like red wine
The sinners wait in line
And we the forgotten can only dream
Of the kind of life we want
Lost in the bayou of boredom

At dawn the dead come back to life
The weeping stops
The living begins
And the reason we started
Is always more important than why we stopped

Deviation

7/9/15

This system
In its wisdom

Has no trap door or
Oblong floor

No God given roar or
Something more

So, I deviate
On one skate

Like a lunatic's mate
Without a wedding date

I dilate my fate
Through a brain that does not wait

What do I do when
Love and matter emaciate?

When the future
Is less than a stalemate?

The screams of this purgatory
Do not relate

I deviate through squares and
Rectangles great

Circles meeting on an island
Much too late

Dirty Paper

This I know
I am made of light and dark
Shadow and sun

Murdering midnight
Finding forgiveness

Green meadow
Wet with winter

Ample sky
Embracing alabaster moon

Justified jazz
Just juking

Alley pregnant
With progress

Night and day
Like the pied piper's stay

Possibility time knows

But we forget

Popes and paupers
Blaming braille

Disturbing Destiny

3/13/15

People tell me that I look like my father's father
My grandfather was more muscular and handsome than
Arnold Schwarzenegger

He wore the Czech army metals
On his General's chest with pride

He left it all behind to lead
The Resistance in World War II

And became such a problem for
The Nazis that he was a
Wanted man

In October of 1944
As the war was winding down
And the allies were winning

The Germans cornered their prey

A gun battle ensued
And my grandfather was murdered

I miss Vojtech Luza every day

Talking to him
Would have soothed and healed me

Now I am an open wound
Searching for closure
That I will probably never find

A love of myself
That my grandfather had naturally

But I take solace in the fact that
Like him
I am willing to die for what I believe

And believe in what I love

Docu Dismal

7/16/15

I saw a documentary
The Best of Enemies
It was called

The film showed
The 1968 television debates
Between William F. Buckley and
Gore Vidal

I saw a little of myself in both men

Conservatism and liberalism
Masculinity and femininity
Brilliance and arrogance

Purgatory and politics
Misery and slothfulness

Caught and told
Bought and sold
Drought and gold

There was so much opinion
It overwhelmed me

Brought me to tears
Gave birth to fears
Until the dust clears

Justice nears
Fawn peers
God hears
Jesus steers

Radomir Vojtech Luza

Dog

8/22/14

No husband
No fiance
No boyfriend
No baby
Dog

God's golden pet
Life's best investment
Time's true keeper

Like pastures and meadows
Dog plays the flute of love
The bass guitar of understanding

Dog, dog, dog, dog
God, god, god, god

Molar in mouth
Centipede in skull
Jury out sick for a year
Mariska Hargitay on crack

All more likely
Than dog leaving

Tom Petty has a dog
I hear
It does not jump
Or bark or breathe
It plays a mean set of drums
Because it is part of his imagination

Like dog is part of mine

And cat is a flat line

Downtown

Open the gates
Let the madness begin

This morning around 9:30
I saw a man eat out
Of a garbage can

Tears welled in my eyes
Like lost tributaries

I could hardly catch my breath
People watched
No outrage
No one seemed to care

Another burden buffaloed
Another heart hardened
Another soul losing its skin

What have we become?
Millions dying
Few trying

In a country with enough food to
Feed the world

Open the heavens
Let the rain fall
The insanity begin

Across from Macy's
A man lost his dignity today to crumbs in a plastic bag

Drunk on Flies

7/1/15

Without purpose
I wonder the highways
And byways of beauty
Like a lost wretch looking for land

The eyes that once saw love
Now embroiled in hate

The ears that only knew music
Now hearing the smattering of terror

The avenues that took in laughter
Now taking in harnessed tears

I am dead to myself
Deader to the world

Drunk on flies
Like a nasty goodbye

Jesus please save me
I am standing on a ledge
Made for less

Jamming jeweled jezebels
With festering fodder

I run until my feet bleed
Into the belly of twilight
Like a wounded wastrel
Gathering midnight in his emaciated arms

East and West

7/18/14

Walls falling
Like broken marriages

Millionaires sipping arrid staircases

Communists and Nazis nesting like gorillas

Twelve times
Anarchy and alliteration

Jesus in the attic
God in the hallway

Computers killing
Drive thrus denying

Museums milking masses
Cylinders subtracting sanity

Breasts barely beginning
Forests freely flirting at 5:15

Subways swallowing sausage
Cathedrals kissing kindness

Perhaps perhaps
There lies love

Yes wrapping its fur
Around your plastic skull like a dead answer

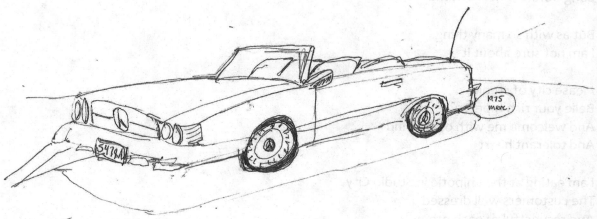

The women walk with a jaunt
As if they know where they are going
As if the sidewalk has not eaten them up

There are black squares on the sidewalk
In Studio City

Each with the name of the
Actors, tv series or movie company on it

I would not mind living in Studio City
Because I had heard of it
Long before it heard of me

But as with so many things
I am not sure about it

Please city of studios
Belie your rich tapestry
And welcome me with open mind
And tolerant heart

I am eating at the Chipotle in Studio City
The customers well dressed
And respectful of each other

Like always
I do not believe I fit in

But the sun is out
My sweater is off
Spring sings in early January
And me along with it

Easy

7/18/15

The beach is within reach
Sky does not ask why
Sun like a pun

Band at hand
Land of sin and sand

Instruments shorn
Like porn
Even horn

Too easy
Existence breezy
Materialism never queasy

Problems come
Like geometry
In theorems times three

Why try when you can buy or get high
Lie in an early grave
For my voice vie

Without an uneven cry
Sorted sigh or
Bitter goodbye

Easy as pie
When you die
With a tie
Like that guy in rye
Who never did fly

Eighth Grade

3/20/15

If you show feelings
You are gay

If you do not
You are macho

I somewhere
In the middle

Feeling to breathe
Loving to believe

Suffocated by self consciousness
Careening confidence

Days are ugly and mean
Like bulleted barbarian

I run to fantasies in my mind
Like rowboat the supple sea

Saliva and sweat
Swelling on a swivel seat
Smelling sweet

Radomir Vojtech Luza

Elvis

Mother and father thought
You were gay at first

All that swiveling and wiggling

But I knew you were Straighter than the cross Jesus hung on

Gospel music unleashing
Man behind mask
Genius ahead of his time
Prince masquerading as king

Comeback TV special in 1968
Proving you were here to stay
Black leather jacket reflecting
Camera glow and female flow

I was on Summer vacation between eighth and ninth grades
In Mountain Home, Arkansas in 1977 when I heard

You dead on the toilet at 42
After going up to go down to go up again

Too young
Too beautiful
Too much still left to give

But not even you were insured
Not even you could escape yourself

Empty Page

11/24/14

The wrist wonders and wanders on empty page
Like therapist does my cranium

It looks and lands
Hooks and sands
A pregnant reptile without hands
I love to write
Nothing I would rather do
Nothing I would rather run to

Opening my palm
To organized mayhem
A languid language of my own
An instinctual integrified loan

God fuels the possibility
With incongruent necessity

Then there is me
With my ego and brawn
Like dissipating yawn

The language is left in the
Backyard under the elm tree

Wafting in the wind
Like a ribald rose

The page is now full
With letter and latitude
Angle and ambiguity

The wrist raining rubies
Under oyster gray sky

Syllable and syntax

But is full better than empty
Something better than nothing

Enough Therapy

I do not need
The picking and pricking
The long days of no sleep
And bitter dreams
The grieving under the heaving
The hypocrisy in all this

Tongue trippers
Charging enough green
To scale a wall
For opinions and analysis
Unique to them

I want straight answers
Not beguiling banter

The truth
Not a Freudian take
On Jung's saunter

A therapist who trusts his instincts
Not an MFA who
Charges to pay for his tuition

Give me poetry as therapy
Not a chair dweller who
Balms his problems
By solving those of others

Putting words in my mouth
Because they do not fit into his

Solutions avoided
By burdening me
With another face
But where is yours
Mr. codebreaker?

Tell me
Will you still talk to me on the couch
When the dollars you are making
Do not equal the love you are taking?

Everyone Altar

8/26/15

Before you
We place the men and women
Of that September Tuesday
14 years ago

The vanishing secretaries and stockbrokers
Temps and tourists
Dying in a time of peace
So we could live

Mothers, fathers
Sisters and brothers
Heroes today
You and me then

Firemen and policemen
Catholics and Protestants
Americans all

No weapons
Only goodbyes

Photographs on the wall
Empty bedrooms by the hall

Taking a fall
A family never to forget
One last call

Hole in heart
Never to start

Healing begins with first step

It is the climb we remember
Not the pay
Humanity on that day

Everything Bagel

I know that ten is larger than nine
Eleven is smaller than twelve
And put together
The two add up to just about nothing

And then there is you
Everything bagel
Scaramouch of sorrow
Trembling teepee of tragedy

End and beginning
My very start to something
On this island of nothing
Continent of convenience
And carelessness

I love your tender hands
And small, shapely feet

The grace with which you carry yourself
And the balance you often telecast
Despite so much imbalance

Those three words, then, of ingrained pain

Trembling hands and harnessed hearts
I love you
I mean each letter of every word
As written and said
Felt and dealt

Face

6/26/15

At 6:26 in the morning
As light finds crevices of your face

God speaks through naked, closed eyes

Cherubic forehead
Still as orange yellow sky

Eyelids brown as chocolate cake
Eyelashes dark as tar

The death of pain
Like loves stain

The hard times getting easier
Without mirth

The angelic nose
Thin raspberry lips
Raised chin

Harmonious day
Beginning anew

Like a Begonia blossoming or
Sun begging

Please my beloved sleep centuries more
If it but brings tranquility transparent

Father Oh Father

I think of your ocean blue eyes at dusk
Tracing the curves of your alabaster face at dawn
Memorizing the thick fingers of your left hand at midnight

You taught me right from wrong
How to sing my song
The way to be strong

The Czech freedom fighter
Who at 19 fought Hitler and
At 25 Stalin

Who gave up political aspirations and dreams
To escape sure death Hammer and Sickle style

Who left country and family behind
With wife and suite case

To run in- between Soviet guard towers and
Climb over Russian barbed wire fences
On the way to Austria and
Political freedom in 1948

You shook the railing around your bed when you saw me
Hours before your death
At that assisted living center
In Montgomery County, Philadelphia
You called home

Father I prayed for you
I stayed for you

The flowers were brighter
On that afternoon you passed away
Than in those lush Bohemian forests
You knew as a lad

Fingers

3/19/15

If the hours
Move faster than the days

And the seconds are
Quicker than the minutes

The fingers of time
Are like cars
On the raceway of rhyme

Banging and breaking
Against crevices and crannies
Trumpets and trombones

Only the sky knows
And symphony understands

I finally stand honest and free
Like a rose without thorns

God pulling one arm
Love the other
I a pauper
Of pillows and puddles

Fire Truck

1/13/15

When I was a boy
I played with a toy fire truck

I wanted to be a hero
And save lives

Love a girl
And rescue her

Embrace my father
And teach him how to love

Hold my mother
And tell her to relax

Reach my sister
And tell her how to follow her dreams

Look in the mirror
And tell myself to have more confidence

When I was a boy
I played with a toy fire truck
Or did it play with me?

Fireworks (Dedicated to Patricia)

7/5/15

In the time zone
Between our breaths

You ignite
The hanging garden of passion
The very face of love

Stepping over
Pockets of oxygen

Stalling under breezes
Of your own making

Underneath vanilla doves
Careening and caressing
The vestibules of declining sin

You enlighten
The angles of my angels

The rudder of
Flags unfurled

As destiny welcomes drama
Titans battle gods and
The July in my mind
Begins at the end
With a bang so clear
It is never loud

A blue streak
Only you can redden

Florida Flora

Hours turning to flowers
Creeping and crawling
In mold of my brain
Like tidal waves insane

On Fort Walton Beach
In Summer of 1987
I went mad

No psychiatrists, psychologists or heavy meds
Jesus and this lad
Bonded bad

Writhing on cross
Wondering why the world
Turns to moss

Between turquoise ocean and vanilla sand
Sitting like mannequin without hands

Heart embalmed
Brain banging on beggar's beef cake
Barbecue banquet
Like dormant dingo digging

23 years and out
Sun does not shout
Broken boy
Moon a ploy

Under rusted rays
Time nor timidity

Only spine of sophistry
On bikini laden shore
Forgotten human lore

Family I do not know
Let go in final blow

On swan white way
Licking peaches to cushion stay

Hard as avocados
Lean as lightning

Difference between reality and the rest
Little bit of light in God's vest

Two weeks of vanquished vacation
Blow to the chest

Dark as STP
The sea
11:03

Come and go like sound
Stay like love unbound

This ferris wheel has an uneven keel
Turning and twisting like an eel

Momma where did you go?
The brows lining your eyes
Have lost their flow

Actress selling real estate
Losing control of fate
Like diamond crushed too late

Pappa who have you become?
Soldier without gun?
Professor oh so numb?

Little sister
Cold as frozen margarita
You blocking you
Like rancid stew

Trio I outgrew
I love you

In Fort Walton
God rides shotgun
On most wicked run

Three against one
Life a machine gun

Streets like asphalt allies
Naked sky
Thunder fly

Run sand at night
Mind takes flight

Moon mellow
As Jell-O

Jackrabbits galloping
Like broken dreams

Piranha with paws
Swimming without laws

Tennis a clay menace

Please judge me not
For like you I am barren

I use words
When actions will do

I fly space shuttles
That explode

And foreign policies that
Beget begot

But nothing prepares me for you
Oh, Fort Walton of black and blue

You kiss the devil
And make him seethe

You reach for the razor
And make me bleed

Football

11/23/14

Before the knees and knives
I breathed your bees and bows
Like an emperor does beaten brows
And Geronimo did open ground

Please leave my Sundays not
You lighthouse by the bay

The children you keep
Helmets you beat
I think of my sister
All skin and bones at ten
Playing pig skin with men

Me diagramming the plays
Like a gridiron master of Zen

I could have played in the league
Could have determined my destiny
Through wins and losses
Points and caught tosses

But the left patella proved problematic
And I had my first surgery at eleven
My father the professor replaced athletics with academics
Now I toil on paper not grass
Looking for the same rhythm to populate mass

God took away a ruby
But gave me a diamond

Let go of the river but gave me the ocean

Veiled and flawed like an exotic dancer
Moving towards the light

Forever Face

The man sitting across from me
At the Coffee Bean on Sunset and Hayworth
Near the Sunset Strip in West Hollywood

In scarred visage and sunglasses
Walking with head down
Hair bouncing on upper back

Short sleeved jungle shirt
Dark camouflaged pants
Flip flops solid and brown

He listening to music through earphones
Muffin, regular coffee on wooden table in front of him

I phone, two small cups of water and inhalers
Take up space on the brown slab

He moves away from me
To get better view of patio

I am relieved
No more deciding whether or not to
Look at him

From now on
I let God choose our paths

Forever Sad

I worry about me
My nervous system and health

How much longer will I grace this gentle planet?

The love I show sometimes
Thrown back in my face
With passion and attitude
Like defrosted chicken

I hardly exercise
I hardly eat right
I just write and eat and sleep it seems

All blurring
All galloping towards each other

In a fatalistic smoke storm
That could end as badly as it began

I need peace of mind
Tranquility
The path
The way

Or what is beautiful
May become forever sad

Fragile Fawn

2/27/15

In the valley beneath your chin
Violins break
Symphonies play
Restraining orders are dismissed

Ballrooms filled
Discotheques stilled

In the mountain range above your sky
Armies collide
Presidents decide
Children abide
Artists reside

In the meadow behind the forest
Juries lie
City councils try

Mothers die
Sisters spy
God cries

Friend

Published in the Altadena Poetry Review

Where were you
In my darkest hours?

During the four mental hospitals
And years with the parents?

I need you like the dawn
On a dusty day

I love you like midnight in May
Words in a play

You larger than life
Poetically musical

Post cards, prayers and pregnant pauses
In the paucity between me and you

If reversed I would have caressed your face
Given you hugs and bloodied pugs

Why were you absent without a clue?
Maybe I had hurt you somewhere too

Friends

3/21/15

Often I wish I had none
The gates of hell would be a pun
Time with you a rusty gun

Smiles and laughter
And awkward glare

Like lice in pastor's hair

The ones close to me
Would not dare

Kicking me in the face
With a flare

Reserved for enemies
In some far off lair

I beg of you God
Do not take them away

As bad as it gets
Without them the end
Would come in May

Radomir Vojtech Luza

Friends

7/6/15

Once you ran through castles anew
Now you pick Satan's brows
Like a boxer does rows

Once the gates of my heart flew open for you

Now the cruise ship to hell cannot cover the swell

Once my tongue wagged for you
Like daiquiri ice cream

Now it sags
Like the end of the day

My poetry stopped singing in early July
Screaming like those towers that dared not stand

Oh, sour fate you stole my love
As you my friend circled above

Full Moon Over Laguna Beach

The medication cannot be missed
For even one day

The music vanishes
If it is not taken

Poetry unfocused
Vision unclear

Steps to the door of the castle
Replaced by ankles
Trees rotten on the inside

They tell me to get off of it
It will break me
Take my talent away

But I walk in the moonlight at Laguna Beach
Staring the future in the face
The past in the back

Words come like spaghetti
Passion like a green forest
And love like a cowboy

Medication leading to synonyms and subjects
Dancing under the full moon
Like wolf on tundra

Illness medicated must be
Insanity at bay
Lingering like salt water
Floating like ice cream on soda

Feet fueling faith
Frolicking fingers feeling like
Free form flowing

Spirit and psychiatrist one

Getting Past It

In this July jail
I find the keys for
August amnesty and
September salvation

I love you
I love me
Together we are free

Both beating bullets
Fired by brazen bullies

I open my eyes and ears
Let instinct illuminate
Gut guide
Intuition inspire

No maybes
Leaping hurdles
Skipping stations
Overcoming obstacles

Time is not on my side
On this merry-go-round

Trembling hands
Tattered pants
Unforgiven rants
Please stop this dance and
Let me off
Without an advance

Girl

I love you Like
no one Before
or after

I need you
Like water
Rice

Thoughts of you
Like mental photographs

Touch tender as a rose
Scent lingering like expensive perfume

I long for you
Like ice cream
Milk
The very reason God created earth

Girl Across From Me at Coffee Bean on Sunset and Hayworth

3/21/15

Left hand on forehead
Sipping medium coffee
Steam rising from cup

Left four fingers
Resting on right thigh

She writes Blonde hair Covering dark
top
Over smallish breasts

Playing with iPhone
Eyes piercing hole
In distance

Black pants
Brown shoes

Silhouetting early evening light
From window behind her

I do not ask her her name
For I belong to another

Blue eyes magnifying thin nose
Red lips pursed over indented chin
The tall young woman places large brown bag on right shoulder
And leaves

God Riding Shotgun

6/16/15

Empty skies
Yogurt clouds

Searching for myself
Through looking glass

Buying love
With actors grin
Alien's sin

Brandishing my heart
With the kind of broken wrists
Only godfathers know and
Poets grow

These musicians out here ain't nothin'
Sliding down rabbit holes for some
Unfocused fame

A name
While looking outside the picture frame

Blood red roses
Striking poses

Underneath the noses
Of the people and Moses
Cleaning cockpit without hoses

Radomir Vojtech Luza

Good Poetry

12/8/14

In the languid waters of this mind
Torture of the word comes first

Like water boarding the syllable
Or denying the noun food or drink

Fight the good fight
Embrace rhythm
Kiss rhyme on the lips

In the fertile soil of this soul
Language is the ground and I am the hoe

I must learn to love myself more
So the poetry can flow through
Me like a tributary a river
Or a bell's chime God's ear

Love myself so good that I will
Always pin evil to the mat of martyrdom
Syntax sent suffering

Gotham my Gotham

8/8/15

Midnight seething like angry octopus
Shadows pouncing from crease to cranny

Trembling palms
Shaking knees
Eyes avoiding eyes
Staying away from primal cries
Like children do flies

I am burned out on poetry
Tired of trafficking verse
Sanctioning syllables

Please big city
Mecca of misanthropes and muses

Touch my hand again and
Show me that shining hill
In the distance

That golden cathedral of
Fallen angels and rising ricochets

Mother Mary
Death flows from
Every crevice
In this turbulent town

I cannot turn
Darkness to light

Take this last flight
Gut my instinct
For an antiseptic fight

Oh, vacantville
Murder me not with
Soldier's boots and 9/11 roots

Your towers and
Scrapers of sky
Cannot buy laughter or a
Prayer for the ever after

Digging dances with ghosts
Burying your able most

Perhaps just once the
Gallows will hang on this very coast
Without so much
As an ample boast

Cement sidewalks and
E train ostrich
To terror tower

Ghosts and galoshes upended
Minnows to masses

Saint Patrick
Would not understand
On that Fifth Avenue

My Fifth Avenue of RFK and the gray way
Madonna's sweater sophistry

East side concrete
West side asphalt
Saks Fifth tolerating tone

Antony and hissing Cleopatra
Times Square tinderbox

Like Burton and Taylor
Dollars on diamonds
World weary
City succumbing
Country caterwauling

Fiction over finesse
Sky sweating
Rain rustling
Between Summer leaves in
Park of grass and grease

American in Gotham
Absolute beginner of
Rhythm and rhyme
Blasphemy and time
Hudson River of blood
Bordering on Jersey of jive

Tears pouring like bodies
Oceans swearing like
Wounded wife

Perhaps tide finds shore
Like wicked step mother and
I Walk 42nd with eyes closed and Belly full

Wandering like a brushfire burning
In this caterpillar of
Shredded wrists and
Condemned hearts

Butterfly of soaring saliva

My New York
Their New York

City of rinse and roll
Plays and tolls

You my breath take
Love make

Like jilted John
Mayor R

You take to give
Give to take

On island of green and growl
Bulls and foul
Garden and Gracie

American in Gotham
Tender as foal

Retinas roaring
Bats breaking in Bronx
Crying like invisible posts
In borough of most

Swollen feet
And stolen heat
In Winter on Northeastern beat

Like prisoners in dungeon
Innocent of crime

Underneath stages and
Words sublime
Another reality

The beaten down souls and
Stretched pore holes
The very sin of the grin

The forgotten and marginalized
Just making it through

Hungry and crippled
Frightened and homeless
Midnight hiding wrinkled face

Blanket covering naked legs
Cart like dart
Sinking heart

God taking holiday
Like cuffed ankles dancing

While we shop at Macys and
Eat at Fridays

Pretending we do not see
Kneeling young and
Grieving stunned
Sitting on edge of eighth

American Gotham
Shining like sun
Falling like star

Alive in city of night
Finally drowning fright

Hand

Your hands I caress
Like skateboards but less

Lips on skin
In a din
A polyester sin

I touch fingers
Like bridges to heaven

When I see the onyx in your eyes
The dawn in your face

Over the mountains
Under the sky

Days are longer
Like eye lashes
Under your brows

The hands of you
Giving birth to vows
My dearest Patricia now

Holdin' On

9/11/15

To the gold in your eyes
Silver in thighs
Ease in lies

When you die
I will not cry
Only wipe the sigh
From the try
That never really
Said goodbye
To the highs in your lows

Tide in your abide
Flowers dotting hair
Diamonds fingers

Still the meadows
In your mind
Ripe and rich

Vibrate with enough pitch
To hold onto any itch
In this wild and wondrous niche

Hole

Ten feet high and
Twelve feet wide

Walls like malls
Is there some other way

When does the giving end
And the taking start

I am always thinking of you
But never of me

Before she died
My mother told me that
I love myself
But I can't find it anywhere

All I feel these days
Is a rat in my gut
Begging me to take a look around

Eating away at my existence
Like a caterpillar a tomato

Drowning in sadness like Bacchus wine

Stuck in the middle again
I know not which way to turn
How many friends I have
Or if family is
Another word for glass breaking

Hollywood

11/23/14

It takes a lifetime to notice
The red shoes
To spot the purple pants of genuine talent

But they lie in Hollywood
Hidden by hand grenades and horseradish
Bulimic billboards
Turkish dream sequences
Student film makers more impersonal
Than their elders

Billie Holiday avenues and boulevards
Detail requiring years to uncover
Minutes to murder

Poems given to simplicity
Pink steps to heaven
Nuance meeting necessity
Headlights careening to carnage

Hollywood city of silent screams
Ville of deadly dreams
River of rust flowing down hillside of history
Horizon hanging heavy

Hollywood Holla

Rappers and scrappers
Van parked for weeks
At the mall

Amplifier for cheap
Take a giant leap

Ballet of guns
And wicked suns

LAPD won't let me be

Dawn's dream
Is dusk's steam

Hollywood and Vine
Vultures peck

Sunset and La Brea
Shopping carts click

Like cargo of cats
Disco of dogs

Silence grows loud
To survive proud

In the distance
Another dream dies
Like fog in my eyes

Hour to Write

3600 seconds left before the Starbucks closes
Before I have to stop writing

The bubbles rise to the top
Of the fish tank
The very entrance to the pool

I am left to wonder what I have lost and
How quickly

Whether the angry mists
And trembling wrists
Have left me stranded
By the side of a busy road

Why I always stand on Mount Aetna alone
Fighting the clouds

"Mrs. Dalloway" stripped me of my confidence
When I was a 22 year old senior
At Tulane University

Why the difference between where I am going and
Where I have gone
Is as thin as a razor blade at midnight
And as thick as the railing of a suspension bridge

With an hour to write
I wonder what will go wrong next

And that alone makes time
As unimportant as ice

As spectacular as love and
As balanced as water

Hurricane

7/7/15

My soul is a hurricane
I have no one to blame
Sin still the same

Walking through the flames
Like a bard without a name

Keep the flowers
Burn the bane

I am alive
To play this game

My soul is a hurricane
Rough as torture
Soft as rapture

It flows and flies
Moves and dies

Tomorrow begins too late
Yesterday opens its own gate

My soul is a hurricane
Burning in the fire of fate
Learning in this dire strait

Wind at my back
Water smack

Hypocrite

7/4/15

I am a hypocrite
Licking yes
While meaning no

Drunk on stop
While accelerating on go

Loving September old
Hating September bold

Maybe time has ears
Listening to trembling thighs
Like mine

Ignoring sighs
Like a divine sign

Singing songs ingrained
Turning down sounds feigned

Broken lives
Spoken dives
Unlike busy hives

Perhaps this purgatory
Serves grand soufflé
In the buffet

Like eggs over easy
A forgiven runaway
On this majestic essay

Radomir Vojtech Luza

I Can't Do It

7/22/15

Time after time
Day after day
I may
But do not bray

Black crows sitting
On edge of bay
Heartbeat bacon
A thousand burdens
As I lay

Cold feet burning
While I stay

In this gay house of fray
As I pray for the kind of hay
Only poets weigh

In the stark corner of now
I shrug
As if the present hardly matters

Knees bend
Head falls
Fingers intertwine

I cannot leave her
I will not go
Trees bend
This cherry orchard of love lends
A corpulent hand

For every exit taken
Journey forsaken

I Do Not Know

11/22/14

The tapestry of good and bad I don't understand
Not any more

The glasses and plates of love
Are too heavy to carry alone

The very God I pray to
Devil I run from
Residing at the same address in my heart

The faith I need often disappearing
Like dew over Dixie at dawn

People I don't get anymore
They say one thing
Then do another

Honesty is a unicorn in the desert of indifference
Oasis nowhere in sight

The art of conversation has been lost
Amid the streaming and sitting
Sending and staring

I awaken from deepest slumber upon realizing
That machines are more important than human beings

Suffering a function not a feeling
And me I do not know
I never seem to soften the blow

These questions I cannot answer
Not this lone dancer

I Do Not Wish To Write

Give the duty to someone else
Who will write what his soul sows
By the end of the day

Let the rich man try
May the pauper cry

Give the passion and pain to
Some unforgiven stain

I will rejoice in the sun
Gallop under the moon

My job is done
Like a robust hun

I flee to myself no more
The chains of disorderly lore

The apples of autumn's store
Given to the closest door
Like an unmolested whore

I stand on mountain's top
Lying in the crack

Begging for smack
I am left with jack
Like a lonely hack

I am too pure for this lack
Instead I rediscover pen and
Mount one more attack

I Don't Speak Spanish

I don't speak the language
I don't understand the accent and ambiguity
But the less I understand the more I comprehend

In its brunette tan and yellow light
Virtue and velocity
Ripe pasture and unwritten narrative
The words capture me like a lassoed llama

I love to listen to Spanish people talk
They twinkle in the dark
Their hard, brown bodies touching the Maker
As they gesture and gesticulate
Arm here
Hand there
Face somewhere else

Eyes piercing hole through the velvet fabric of the sky
The very knees of God
Elbows of industry

All I know is Ne se hable Espanol

All I know is I wish I knew more

I yearn to know the tender refrains of Hispanic history
How they came to California
Why the city of Angels has a Spanish name
And why oh why the best Laker and Dodger fans speak Spanish as their first language

I wish I spoke Spanish
I wish Spanish spoke to me

From the burned out barrios of East LA
To the bronze sidewalks of Downtown
To the flashing police lights of North Hollywood

Traffic jams of metal and mud
Spider webs of sugar and string
Sinking battle ships of my own making

I loved you once my Spanish dove
But that was long ago
In a world populated by ferries and sprites

Hair dark as Hitler's final solution
Eyes brown as tree bark
Hands soft as Guatemalan fish

You as beautiful as the language you speak
The tongue you leak
The syllables you seek

I Left My Heart in New York City
(and I'm Not Sure I'll Get It Back)

8/19/15

The sun comes at you from an angle
In early August
On West 47th between 7th and Broadway

TKTS booth looking out of place
On edge of Times Square
With red awnings and state-of-art design

Ecuadoran, Italian, Peruvian, Dominican and Puerto Rican
Eating at same table at diner on West 49th and 8th

Police siren, car alarm and horn
Piercing tranquil
Summer night
Like rat bag of garbage
On side of road

If love had a name it would be Manahatta
Hand like paper towel
Heart guided missile
Eyes like strobes surrendering
Ears garden thickening

You are sustenance and solidarity
I celebrate you
From Hudson to the Heights

E train of blood and bone
42nd to financial district

A train
Cloisters to Columbus Circle

Times, Lincoln, Herald and Union Squares of
Sweet feet and full hands

Central and Madison Square Parks
Of bent heads and Summer gazes

Radomir Vojtech Luza

Greenwich Village, Chelsea,
NoHo, SoHo, Uptown, Downtown
And Midtown dot the map of
Steady arms and swift legs
East side angst

West side banks
Broadway pranks
Harlem ranks
Yankees sank
Knicks tank

My soul belongs to the
Island of cloud scrapers

Borroughs of age, sage and page
Suburbs of planes and ports

Lady of war and score

I gave my heart to New York City and
I hope I never get it back

I Wanna Die

Happiness is the truth
Death is for poets and lead singers
Torture is teacher
Words God
Language heaven

Fences I did not climb
Mountains I have put in the way
Detours I did not take
Opinions like bark

You escaping like water
The genius in those hazel halogens
Burning a hole through frozen handshakes

Putting me before you
When you are the one thing
I would die for

The end has no answer

Ice Blended

The snow beneath me
Is black with soot

My naked feet are red
With blood

I want to run
But I do not know where

I want to laugh
But I do not know when

I want to caress a woman
But I have forgotten how

The ice beneath me is thawing

I fall like an anchor
Into the ocean

I must save myself
Swim to safety

This time there is no one to save me
This time love is a dream

If

It hurts like rain on alabaster dove
This breaking of my poetic wrist

This curling of my divine tongue

It pokes a hole in the
Carpeting of my brain

The very surface of my soul
The tender tundra of my heart

Why write verse
If they do not gather to listen
Only hear

If the instruments of God are missing

If what is closest to heaven
Is turned into what is nearest to hell

If I Was Black

Flowers I would fold
Tales mold
Abortions put on hold
Crack pipes not have sold

Disability checks foretold
For more than black skin behold

To policemen not be cold
Perceptions change
Reflections rearrange
Time strange

Art is bold
Politics gold
In society not do as told
Rather as polled

Slavery wrong
Sing it in song
With beer and cheer
Without fear and sneer

Immigrant

3/10/15

The Czech parents
Accents like anchors
Armor like ash

What I feel
I do not say

What I say
I do not feel

When it hurts
I steal the real

When it rains
The soil does not heal

Black and blue
I the outsider
Run to walk

Sauntering down
Blue bird way
Only to see the black

That never took the time
To know my lack

2

Immigration Alley

Maybe if you had seen
The town I came from
The house I lived in
You would understand

If you saw bloated bellies
And trembling palms
Every day all the time

You would know
I am a human being
Not a trash receptacle

I do not want to break any rules
But I want a chance
At life in America
Like you have

Is that so much to ask?
Is that too much to believe in?

I want my family to live in peace
I do not want to be poor any more
I want to be free

Anything less, after all, would be un-American

Imposing

7/4/15

Drunk on traffic
The hours expand like a gulf's shore

I am imposing
They say
Beyond lore
Above the family store

I impose
On those who
Let themselves be imposed upon

Lying at the beach
Like a forgiven leach
A voyeur
Looking at not for sex

In the adult section
Time takes a vacation
Like a loner on parade
A stoner on the fade

Impose myself on the sales clerk
He laughs when I do
The rest of the crew
Not feeling new

This bipolar giant
Despising violence
Disguising ambulance to New Orleans
While embracing assonance

Radomir Vojtech Luza

Infected by Love

Dining on this supper
Of perfect hugs

Brunching on the dessert of
Instant love

This time daddy
I am not waiting
For you to abate

Only sit by the river with
Rod and bait

Like an acting teacher without weight

A messy hand
That cannot stand

I am leaving L.A. yesterday

Abdicating this bloody throne
Like a lion
Its righteous home

Eating breakfast
Near the lake
Where Cleopatra
Ate her cake

Lunching on a feast where
Marc Anthony had the least

Ironic Island

7/9/15

I sit inside my 2012 Toyota Prius
Near midnight

At the Ventura Place shopping center
In Studio City

A young woman in a short blue skirt and top
Lights a cigarette
As soon as she gets in her car

The lithe lass soon drives off
Like the lead car
In the Indy 500

In no time flat
Two police cars
Quickly drive by

Lights flashing
Sirens wailing

Life is hard
Even in Studio City

Days are long
Even among the rich and famous

Poetry I write
This late at night

A few people walk
Into the Vons Supermarket
And leave early

A guy sits in front of Panera Bread
Then leaves

Irrigation Alley

The asthma of love
Cannot be ignored or
Easily contained

It meanders highways and byways
Only God knows
Like a rollicking rhino

Heaving and coughing
The illness spreads like Winter and
Panhandles like a wino

Treading fragile ground
It bites and bites
Like a nasty albino

The asthma of love
Has been a disease for centuries
As we tread lawns and
Fondle arabesques
Not of our own making

This sickness
This follicle of fondness
Leaps and lacerates
Like an uncommon lariat

Loosening lips and
Landing on lunar landscapes
Befitting badges of ebullient beefcake
Loading larynxes
Like liquid larva

It Girl

7/15/15

Who are you?
Why are you?

Beauty on the outside
Skin deep

Love on the inside
Another leap

Deborah Kerr
Ingrid Bergman
Jennifer Jones
Grace Kelly
No naked pictures
No media disgrace

Oscars all
Heaven's call

Talent matters
Inside out
God spout

Sex dies young
Then you're strung

Sadly sung
Without a lung
Or tongue
On a rung
Terribly hung

It Is What It Is

7/14/15

In the corners
Of this hotel room

Fingers and capillaries
Of desperation
Find a hold

No wife
No father
Dead mother
Deaf sister
Frightened cousin

The cage has room number and
Early morning maid service

A bed for two
That one will use and
Wi-Fi for a laptop
Out of use

In the crevices
Time makes no sense

Love has an expiration date and
The difference between
Here and there
Is a 727 from Times Square

Jingle Jangle

1/13/15

Nerves tangled like electric chords
The court of appeals will not leave me alone
My best friend keeps hanging up the phone

I am thinking of stopping therapy
Quivering lips
Blood in the sink
Trembling stomach
No one can make me do something
Unless I choose to do it

The politics in my blood have been drained
Like a river during a heat wave

I am not sure I want to make it to tomorrow
Giving up is easier

Fear is a mirage
I use as an excuse

I walk in my father's footsteps
Dead without your thin arms
Around my thick waist

John

Imagine the sky yellow and blue
The meadows sprinkled with dew

Your eyes covered with quite a
Different hue

My feet walking down a crowded avenue

When you were murdered in 1980
I skipped Ms. Reuter's senior science class to attend a
Memorial down New Orleans way

Your words and music spoke to my being

My little Czech soul like unicorn prancing
In hell's harvest

Open my skull John and get your lyrics out

Close my ears and they still
Hear that carnation of a voice that vanilla swan of a wit

Welcome to your tea party the one in Central Park

Under all those trees where the soil is ripe with cobbled imagination

And the blackbird flies in the dead of night

John Again
(Dedicated to John Lennon)

Bird flying too close to the stars
Wings burned by orange moon

Half of my whole
The bread to my soul

Crying while lying
Bleeding while proceeding

If if were real
Your eyes would belong to God
Your ears Mother Mary

Licking stamps made of wine
You travel no line

Like indigo warrior
Chasing hook

We got the
Strawberry look

Hair in your face
Murder a disgrace

You went
Like you came

Quickly and loudly
Only you would have imagined
Something else

Jose

7/18/14

Dark meadows
Dungeons through eyes

Clouds never built lies

Shadows whistling whispers

Tongue tired of tart tomato

Lying back
To bone

On mattress of misery
Dollars tied to
Bloody beginning

Day rolls nine
On wheel of line benign

Children hanging
By neck at recess

Jamming mind
Into soul

Driving jester
Into king's hole

Kennedy

Keep the conspiracy theories and
Multiple shooters
Oswald acted alone

It does not matter how this President died
What matters is how he lived

Redwood rising
Bunyon weeping
Tarzan leaping

Eyes seeing into next century
Like retinas roaring

No Vietnam
Civil Rights rectifier
Astronaut amplifier
Camelot Camembert

Perhaps he cheated
But I don't think he meant to hurt

From U-boat to
White House

Living for something bigger than himself
Loved the children
Cherished America

Kennedy curse
Heard in reverse
In midnight hearse

Those who talk
Never wanted to see him act

Key

9/10/15

Key was given to me
By a nameless breeze
On its knees

I am free
To be

Like rose petal
Heavy metal
Greg Nettles at third base
In the Bronx

He would never settle
For a tin kettle

When steady palms and
Sturdy knees
Find gentle rental

Appetite for Lentil
Alabaster dental
Bruce Lee mental

Killing Verse

Killing poetry is easy

Shut down the
Boulevard to your dreams

Before slicing the wrist
Of the imagination

Murdering rhyme is easy
Shoot the syntax, subject and syllables
In the head
Before erasing the alphabet of the heart

Kill vocabulary of the fingers
Suffering of the soul
Tomahawking the tears of the tender

Vacuuming mistakes and matter
Power washing vows and victories
Poisoning the holy and sacred
Gassing grace
Beheading the bullied
Steam cleaning toil and truth

Do not step into that river
Of sweat
Until it becomes an ocean of blood

LA FOUND

I found it in Echo Park
I found it in the dark
I found it in the mad mad bark
I found it in the dead chicken hawk
No more broken lenses will he stalk

I found it in the devil's store where he sells bibles for ten cents and more
I found it in NOHO's flair

I found it in Silver Lake's glare
I found it on Wilshire's eight
Where even the rich are late

And the red cred carpet wears its mate in this silly silly city always bait
I found it in Griffith Park Shakespeare in the Summer dark
I found it in Chavez Ravine where the ghosts of Brooklyn's past are silenced with every broken bat

I found you there on Sunset and Vine where fairytales walk without knives

I found it there in every star where Bill Hailey sang to every car

I found it in Melrose's eagle's nest
I found you there in Toluca Lake in Burbank's distance and Glendale's face
I found you in Van Nuys' falling lips and in Los Feliz where the House of Pies licks my loins like
The city council lies

And down in Malibu and Pacific Palisades Barbra Streisand rides her giraffe in the shade

I found it at Zuma
I found it at Venice
Riding like the morning along Ventura

I found it in every homeless man and woman
I found it in each traveling luggage bag
Maybe a thousand a week we have

I found it in the torn tennis shoe
I found it in the shelters on Slaughter
And the bronze sidewalks
Downtown that at five in the morning make me weep like a dead man
When the 204 takes me to hell's door

Just 100 black men and me
Out at 6 in at 6

I sleep outside as I look for work
And get in at 8:30

The 101 in the Summer squeezes right like the lions making movies and music here in lapid angles
Like these green mountains along the 134 to Pasadena mothering and fathering me to a wide
Open laugh
Only the hymns of life could get from this barren lack

But mainly I find you in the streets
In the air where the people are frightened
But they don't dare to care
     •
City of Angels mother of the misbegotten
But children know the truth when they see the gray
Angels feel the light when they feel the day

God is Los Angeles
It is in his sun drenched hair

LA LA Lost

9/4/15

Near Capitol Records
In old Hollywood
Vine Street no longer matters

Its cursive path and
New math
Add to subtract

The new Starbucks on Sunset Boulevard
Is alive tonight with
Green haired dolls and
Bare-chested falls

The big Bank of America
On the corner
Is home to sleeping bags,
Rag dolls and a few eyeballs

The Walgreens across the street
Shines like some beacon on the hill
It was once a Border's Bookstore

People count
Not architecture

Faces not races
Braces not vases

In LA light is water
It drowns every daughter
Like fodder

Radomir Vojtech Luza

you rock, rock ~ Forest

LA You Don't Play

Never has there been a boy
Who crossed your drug dappled streets
Your bullet bullion neighborhoods
Your paranoid peacock policemen

Like this boy
Torn and twisting in the
Pacific panhandles of purgatory

Like a night at the Roxy
After the band leaves
At the Comedy Store
Before the egos exit

Sometimes I board at the
Back of the orange bus
Where the children sleep
And the poets die

Slumber does not last
In the underbelly of
Rhythm and rhyme
Sasquatch and time

Maybe by dawn
Light slips into the river
Around Studio City

Where I got on in the first place
And the wisdom I once had
Overtakes that which I have learned

Lankershim Lights

Lemonade lubricates at Pitfire Pizza while I
Flourish among the flora, flannel and frolicking fairies
Like an emperor elevating esoteric

I watch the movie screen at Laemmles NoHo
Like a guru guiding Gandhi

At Panda Express
The orange chicken is as sweet as the sun
And as mellow as Maui

The beautiful burrito at
Chipotle Is more beatific than
Bjorn Borg's Blizzard of a backhand

At Big Wangs Kobe Bryant is on ten screens
And it is still not enough

Supper at Vicious Dogs is a salient salute to sauerkraut at sunset

After I have rehearsed with my band at Amp
Like Ozzie oozing alabaster orb

I go to Bob's Espresso Bar
To mix with metaphysical mop tops
And mingled masterpieces

Like music wafting across the horizon
I feel the night build and bend
Trembling at the knees
Like a lovelorn prince looking for his Cinderella

I discover the deity in the details
The very fingers that mold hands and caress cherubic faces

The Federal Bar finds me
Arcing towards 2 a.m.
Like a panther politely parking his paws in paradise

This Lankershim Boulevard
This corner of my consciousness

This bouquet of flowers on my birthday
This very stone's throw from Hollywood

This 101 wonderland
And red line ricochet

This reason for God's reason
Apprehended and analyzed
Like a murder suspect

Like the very grab at grace
We get but once

Staring at the moon
At 3 a.m.

Orange yellow with asphalt lips

Lankershim lights in my dreams

Lankershim lights in my afternoons

Lankershim lights
Spreading across my midnights
And pregnant bites
Only you can stop the polluted fights

And illiterate flights of these muddied nights
Like ambitious kites

My dear sweet
Lankershim lights

On Lankershim Boulevard
I found myself

The rebel and the roustabout
The soldier and the scoundrel

The night tossed me into your orbit
Your very river of regret
Lake Placid of ribaldry

I, the Sir Lancelot of leprosy
The wolf of this whirlwind

The avenged angel on this avenue of acoustic alliteration and accreting illumination

Nearly died to live again
Almost cracked to crumble
On your cement sidewalks and October breezes

Like a marathon runner
Stopped still in his tracks
Head beneath axe

A running back without football
Not aware of the facts

But you saved me Lankershim
Cupping palms
And breathing confidence into confidence

Like a shark
Who discovers that he really is a dolphin

Or a boy who finds that special girl to share the rest of his days with

You bought me the mountain to maneuver
The very lights to shine on my wooden cross

Leader

7/12/15

I am a born leader
Meant to show the way
Lover of the law
Massager of imagination

Put the two together and
Politics is art

People like the way I talk and
Walk and do not balk

They are enamored
Of my presence and stature

I am a people person
I need others around me

Walking door to door
In a grass roots campaign
Victory I will not feign
Losing is my bane

Realistic I must remain
In a state of political nirvana
Yet I am frighteningly sane

In the end
I do not bend for friends
But a helping hand lend or
Scar mend

Hugs, verse, and dealing with thugs
I heed
Like a done deed

I am born to lead
Willing to need
Feeling the pull of greed
Beneath the fallen steed

Radomir Vojtech Luza

Leaving LA

In the Spring of this Summer
I want to bolt
Leave LA for good

I have seen too many
Comedy Store cowards
And addicted comedians
To last 11 lifetimes
Bi sexual barbarians

The superficial auditions
And puppet agents
That show up for a price
All over town

And still the actor suffers
As he is not guaranteed anything

Take advantage of the weakest link
I wish to leave LA
Its mismatched outfits and
Paranoid pornography

Its one percent success rate and 99% failure margin
That puts so many on the street

Dreams die hard on Hollywood Boulevard
Aspirations are asphyxiated
Like birthday balloons

I want to exit this city of
Gangs and ghettos
For something better
If utopia comes without a price

Or maybe I should be strong
And see what I started through

Libuse

The name ringing in awkward
Agony and allure
Czech nation balancing on its beam
Like an aimless azure

Time stinging deeper than
A year's mistakes

And the moss grows on your
Walls full of grace and gargoyles
Jesus and java juice

Antigone at your door
Hitler at the midnight shore
Still you left it all behind
And gave us all a riper mind

Laughter leaping like
Leaning lizard

Instincts and beauty few knew
Except for those evenings in the kitchen
When you shared the trials and triumphs with me
Love dripping from your hips
The silver surfer riding your
Mane and me in awe of your
Golden bane like Lancelot the
Forest's sun

Peace in those brunette eyes
Never telling lies
Your gravity flies

Light

6/17/15

On the eighth day of
The eighth sun

In the eighth domain
I slept

The sun at my feet
The moon at my waist

No poetry
No presumptions
No pickles in a jar
Meant for fingers

Dreams come
Days went
Diaries disappeared
Like electrons
From a computer screen

Jesus came
And went

Judas was forgiven
Jezebels danced with juju bees

I lay on a bed of down and counted the sheep
As they leapt

Upon opening my eyes
The blessed alabaster orb shone like
A prince with his prize

Eros of Angels

167

Like Crazy

7/14/15

I am going crazy again

Leading with the left
Following with the right

Writing takes me away
From talking shadows and
Dark brown meadows

3 am backyards
Midnight front yards

Bloody palms and
Forgotten psalms

I am going mad
Like a lunatic without a hospital
A nut in a rut

Past melting with present
Now and then
Like half a hen

Polluting my giddy hose
Like a pair of nasty foes

Wrists ripping at the front door
But the back says more

Blood flowing
In bedroom nightmares
Like ten ton grizzly bears

Little World

The fire has been doused
The rain collected

I tire of my little world
And its narrow corners

My tiny universe and its
Pockmarked alleyways

Poetry rusts
Talent drowns
Love ricochets off the radio transmitter

Nothing happens just like that
Nothing worthwhile anyway

Take my unbalanced balance
And black bottom line turned red
To the sea
With debris

A new form to start perhaps
With social and cultural banter

But through it all
I remain myself

Like a bear hibernating
A gazelle galloping
A lion leaping

Altering this milky marble
Like sun to moon

Where wrong numbers
And harassed hearts
Turn Autumn leaf brown

I move on
Like unicorn rising

Arm to hand
Crowd to band

Little world take flight
To island of light

Listener

7/10/15

My little listener
Round and round you go
Never stopping

I squeeze the pimple
Of my existence

You open your ears and
Take it all in

No ego
No bravado
No whispering lamp post

You simply are
What you are

Be what you be

Take when you take
Give when you give

Let the rest of us be
Because somehow you see
The broken waves
On this ocean of unmitigated raves

Please my dearest Patricia
Listen to me for one more day

Your sky will be less than gray
Thunderstorms held at bay
Hurricanes ceasing in May

Los Angeles

You frighten me
Dearest city of now

Red carpets and flashbulbs
I do not want

Mismatched outfits
Industry banter
Unrealized potential scare me

To need fame is to devour it

To love you City of Angels is letting go and
Letting you steer my train

My brain is amiss after divorce and
Move to you
City on the ocean

Only now am I beginning to pursue
What I want at the speed I want

To love myself after a decade
Of driving on
The wrong side of the interstate

The balm to bathe my bruised soul in
My heart's tender caress

If I went through what I did to get to you
Sweetest tinsel town

You must be
The magic
I was looking for

Love

Love as real as an aching back
Wounding but not breaking
Breaking but not killing
Killing but not raping
Raping but not molesting

May the younger generation stand up
Love comes easy to them
Like shooting an arrow
Or sleeping naked

It is not Shakespeare
But Shangri La
Not Tolstoy or Dostoyevsky
But tango and dice

Adoring the adoration
Swimming in the flow
Like eels in the 4 am tan
Or real estate agents in the Sunday stretch

Love as authentic as words
Withdrawn and wounded
As water between willows

Love and Hate

11/22/14

If love guides golden canaries
Hate stands on the shoulders of children
Begging for discipline their weeping parents cannot afford
Their better natures do not allow

Love stands upright in the middle of a wicked storm
As naked and strong as the sun

Hate bends over its own elbows in the back of a bus
Cobbling together fabric and fashion
For a coat of bloody colors and mistaken identities

Love is a metaphor for God
Hate a synonym for less

For in the long run
Love is an eagle
Landing on high
Hate a vulture dying in Death Valley

Our soul both parts dawn and dusk

Love kisses the universe's lips
Hate hell's hips

Maybe Maybe

The swing curling
Is not hurling
A power worth sterling

Like some lonely bat
Which sat on a hat
Without a black cat

Children have the power
Of Greek olives in a pungent salad

Sitting beneath the Mona Lisa
All my strength released
Like tigers breached

I often ask God
Why I am so low
Then so high
Without a balance
That comes so slow

He never answers
But to say
It is what it is and
Always will be

He stares in my direction
As if I am dust
Yet he knows of the angelic rust
In the heavenly must

Mc Donald's on Ventura Boulevard
in Studio City

3/16/15

The flailing begins
Before you enter the double doors

Before the opinion you have of yourself
Differs from that others have of you

Before anger subsides and
Comprehension begins

The children here
Walk in darkness
Lost upon their parents
Unlit cigarettes dangling from lips
Limping toward oblivion
Taking sidewalk and symmetry away

Like lepers without a dream
Cannibals with a loud scream

In Studio City
Shadows sashay in the
Sad storms of silence along
Mary Tyler Moore Boulevard

Laughter is an eel slithering through the rivers and
Avenues of this commercial break of a town
Lost in asphalt and angel dust

Me

I am beginning to like me
All commas and apostrophes
Mostly Shakespeare and Hemingway

Living through this rusted day
I am starting to appreciate me
All subjects and clauses

Mainly Dvorak and discipline
And the kind of lows only my highs know

I am loving myself more these days
Holding back the avalanche of acrid alliteration

Moving forward on the clear sky sanity of the promised city
Forgetting the vanquished vowel of vanity

I am speaking up more these days
Secrecy no longer a floating carp
But an avenue away from the
Crowded chaos of my closet

Mental Hospital

Confusion bending door knob
Frustration caterwauling through these thick walls

Mandeville state psychiatric facility in 1987
I did not think I would get out

Mind thrashed like scrambled eggs
Blood tests at six in the morning in the cold

Medications stuffed down my throat
Like vanilla rocks
Five guys to a room
Structure docks

Without permission of psychiatrist
I do not get out

On day of release
I am feather wafting
Grown man crying
Batman flying

Did the stay help? A little

Was it worth it? Probably not

Should father, mother and sister
Be held responsible for putting me there?
Yes and no

26 miles in back of cop car
Along longest bridge in country
Cuffs on wrists and ankles
Trembling hands
Shaking legs

I need to take some responsibility myself
Love there was through guarded tongues
Metal lips

Mess

I like a nice mess
Family is a good guess

Sashaying and swaying to the
Beat of neat
The anticipated orange grass of comfort

I run to the river
Walk to the stream
Gallop to the gulf
Crawl to the ocean

To witness the mess from distress
The angelic howl of mistake
The claws of candy

A good mess is a new dress
Covering crannies and crime

Old stress
Infusing disco and dime

My mother's guess
Never wrong
Merely a new address

Michael
(Dedicated to Michael Hutchince of INXS)

12/5/14

I bet you wrote in coffee shops
Until they noticed you

Words
Short and cursive

Curls
Long but never abusive

Australian charm
Vaunted alarm

It took ten mountains to bring you down

But when you went
Hanging on the hotel door

The universe trembled
Like a bludgeoned cow

You had us moving right
When you moved left

Light on
Bright lamp

You will shock us again some day
When open palms meet closed fists

And your pen is greater than the devil's den

Midnight Light

12/5/14

The keys to the puzzle are black and white
Like day and night

Giving to get
Getting to give

Some days are darker
Light is too hard

Tunnels over beaches
Funnels over screeches

Laughter comes easy
Death is the third act
Following the childhood and moon

Climbing the elm tree to ripe pasture
Fertile field

Life is yellow orange sun
Swinging open to accommodate the one

While we stand waiting for grass to grow
And inches to mow
Rubies can be slow

Midnight Mass

7/3/15

In the alters and alleyways of affection
The dalliances and doorways of love indent

Like kisses on the back of the neck
They dance to and destroy
The very fruit they nestled in the forests of fear

Do not tell me that I am good
Tell me how to get better

Do not say that you care for me
Show me

Caress the cheeks of the Messiah
Like David slingshot

Romeo his Juliette
John water bottom

At 12 o'clock
Dust and dawn collide
Like fortunate scarecrows

In the hills above the city
Where dust and drink
Meet like a gregarious cacophony
Of belly filled lunatics

The fools at midnight mass believing in God
Jesus coming back
Like a poet in a meadow of
Metaphors and magic

Midwestern Boy

Eyes that prick sky
Like curved lie

Bending and breaking
Little fly

How do I know you?
Puzzle in cut off jeans

Skin peppered by LA lights
Brain rollicking hills

Lips quivering like cold hamsters
Hands shaking like torn blisters

Maybe air here
Is not like air there

Tattered and torn
Thin fingers

Ten fold giving
Ten fold taking

Mind Open

Finally the brain is bilging
The mind mandating new mildew

And I who once sat on the corner
Now sit on a throne of platinum and gold
Constructing rhyme from nothing but time

Unclogging the pipes
Learning to relax
Coming down to earth

It does not all have to rhyme or slam
Be alliteration or assonance

It can simply be me and you
Hand in hand
Walking down the beach

Sky in my eye
Love from above

Mirror, Mirror

My mother watches reruns of Big Valley
She says that her favorite actor on the show
Is Lee Majors

If the occasion was right, she tells me,
She would marry him

We watch him on the Six Million Dollar Man
I consider having a bionic stepfather

This box of glory
This box of shame

Like bees to honey
Fingers to money

A pastor's flame
Beggars name

Oh solace
Oh fame

Oh desert
Oh same

Mister Fantastic
(A Tribute to Robin Williams)

Falcons landing near your flame

Drunk on love

Good religion sewn onto your sleeves

Even God sweats and grieves

Like a languid language
Lost in luxurious lingering

Eyes as blue as buildings
As true as endings

I want to be you
Drowning in now

An addict's row
Like a tarantula's hoe

Head first into black snow

Like a Latin lover
With a tainted rainbow

Molesting the Bard

I saw a play last night
That would have made Shakespeare
Die another death

Macbeth was raped and abused
Like a mongrel
On the side of the road

The idea behind the play
Sacred and beautiful
Aborted with a twirl
Of the director's wand

I sat in front row
Head down
Eyes moist as rain
Heart palpating like drum

Why make a whore
Out of Lady Macbeth?

Why set the play
In an insane asylum?

Why stage the play at all?
If it does not break my fall?
My voice a pall
In a universe that does not stall
Heeding my call

Moments

The dirth of passion
The subtraction of Spring
Bring me to you
And the queens you bring

Checkmating the alleys
And avenues you call your own

The very canyons and cliffs
Criss crossing this town of
Flashbulbs and red carpet ifs

I loved you once so long ago
I barely remember the whys and wherefores

Only your apartment by the University of New Orleans
Where we walked at six in the morning
On that first Saturday I visited you

Just to go back to bed
Awakening amid an octopus of arms and elbows

The manipulation of Mars
The division of divisiveness

You talked about the Beatles
And how unique they were

I about vulnerability and the courage it requires

Do you ever think of me?
For I will always remember you
Like a moment in the malleable madness of midday
Your eyes burning hole through my skin

Your dark raven hair and tissue touch
Complimenting my manhood like Bacall did Bogey
Or my mother my father

The check still has not cleared
But I wonder once more where

Moon

I went walking on the moon
Without a spoon
To taste a dune

The stomach was full
Brain agile
Fingers nimble

I went walking on the moon
Like a goon
Roughly hewn

Sun in the distance
God above

I laced up the boots
Started to skate
Through the gate
But got there late

I went walking on the moon
Much too soon
Like a loon
In late June

When I got there
I realized
The moon looked
Like a poem
I wrote before noon
To my own tune

Mother Speaks

If mother was alive
She would be 85

Old enough to be dreaming of mountains
But falling down hills

Scaling Everest
But screaming at K2

She would probably tell me
That she has never loved me more

Time and temerity add to talent

Jousting with joy leads to jealous jezebels

She would look me straight in the eyes and blink

Proving once and for all
That to be alive is to be imperfect

To die alone is to remember to forget to care

She would hold my trembling hands in hers
And sing me an old Czech lullaby
And I would know what heaven must be like

Mother Maybe

On this ghostly inferno of snow and sun

Planet in disrepair
Orb without hair

I search for oasis of glass
On island of hefty mass

Treading lightly on the shore
I see my sister in the door
Near my cousin on the floor

My father sleeps a gentle nap
My mother always at his back

I the virtuoso of the pack
Snap mental photos on the run

Knowing not larynx from lip
Gateway from hip

Healing scars that rarely speak
At this unearthly leak

Is this heaven? Is this hell?
I only dread what I cannot sell

Movie Marlin

8/24/15

At the Coffee Bean on
Sunset and Hayworth near the
Sunset Strip in Hollywood

Two guys talk loudly
About producing a film in Wyoming
Two boys with bucks in a boat
Tackling tundra like tea

Giving them my name and email address
They say they will get in touch
With more information

One writes
The other directs
Together they impress

Both producers on this feature film
The scribe asks if he can
Look me up on line

I say yes
Holler peace as director in jeans and red top
Walks out glass door

Knowing chances of hearing from them again
Are thin and none

My Mojo

I thought my mojo was
As dead as Abraham Lincoln

As quiet as a Southern night

But it now licks the sun
And eats the moon

It loves because
It chooses to

No matter the hurdles
Or broken fingernails

My mojo has returned
As if it never left

As if the possibilities
And probabilities
Were certainties

And the arms on me
Could lift my dreams
With the strength of Hercules
And the wisdom of Plato

My mojo is back
Stronger than a Japanese tsunami
Quicker than Muhammad Ali
In his prime

My mojo is not coupled with yours
Together we own paradise
And run along the tracks
That once saw us divided
We multiply in the summer air

Like two beach balls on vanilla sand

Nectar of Now

Frozen smiles laughing
Like broken ice

Jamming jukebox
With posed voices

Leering at children
Love on vacation
Like gazelle never outrunning tiger

Donna Summer playing
In the background
Billie Holiday
In the foreground

Different styles
Sounds that you
Do not have to try to hear

Who cares about addiction
How about passion
Conviction?

Thick cars
On a narrow street
Dead voices
Living ears

Always then
Forever now

Tie the two together
Tongues wag
Eyelids do not sag
Salt water dares not drag

New Orleans

I often think of your
Sunken cemeteries and drunken carnivals
Before I go to sleep

Your comedy stages and theatres
Once of such import
Now dead along with my parents

I pray to you Big Easy
Your winding French Quarter paths
And Uptown alligator shirts

You are my history
But not my present

My Cowboy Mouth
But not my golden tongue

Friends
You gave me a few
But not enough

I wish I had the talent
To traverse your tapestry
Or even explode on your excess

But I am a humble poet
Who loves you Crescent City
Despite the cruel lads in high school
And the manipulative theatre directors

For you gave me Tulane University
The best four years of my life

My mother and the love she spread
Like brush fire before
Her untimely death

Mardi Gras beads and doubloons
You brought like
A yearly pilgrimage up K2

New York Blue York

8/20/15

Under the noses of Fifth Avenue shoppers
Sits a young man
In tattered, dirty t-shirt and tennis shoes
On cement sidewalk

Holding a card reading
HOMELESS, EMBARRASSED AND ASHAMED
LOOKING FOR MONEY FOR A TICKET HOME

Spare change sparkling in open cap
Under late afternoon
Mid Manhattan sun

Saks Fifth Avenue, H and M and American Girl shopping bags
Hovering over his head
Like fruit on a branch

I ask why and how
A hundred times

It never rhymes
Amid the sea of dimes

Has this boy committed crimes?
Like Jesus hated moral mimes

New York City

The Path train to 34ᵗʰ Street from Northern New Jersey
I miss
Like a dagger to the heart

9/11 murdering peace of mind
The F train I contemplate
Whenever the need to outweighs
The need not to
All homeless people and
Burned out executives

Times Square
Skyscrapers and Toys R Us store
Like mannequins from the past

Starving actors without coats in Winter
Broadway haves and have nots

Knock me down
Like goldfish bowl does guppy
Rat poison roach

I could not breathe
Think or love

Ex wife feeling
My tantrums and tainted dreams
Like egg leaking

New York City no longer
The only place for me
The end of the beginning

Gotham City
You did not answer my prayers

The living room of
The second floor apartment
Of 36 Liberty Avenue
In the Journal Square section
Of Jersey City

A war zone

Cage with no way out

Until guilt and shame be damned
I flew the coop
With just enough confidence
To never land again

Ego finally making guest appearance
Self esteem running interference

747 to West Coast

After eight years
Brain unscrambled enough to love again

No Family Blues

3/22/15

I have one cousin in this country
A sister that does not talk to me

And a family in the Czech Republic that
I have not seen in 23 years

I spend most of my days
In front of the laptop
Or writing poetry

But not with the people I love
The people that would heal my
Scars and make me whole

The chasm grows every hour
But I do little or nothing to
Narrow the ocean between who I am and who I want to be
Who I was and who I will be

Because pain is an easy way of delaying the truth
And the path to that truth may be more
Than I am willing to traverse

No Plan B

Putting dreams and schemes
In one apple cart
Like beating heart

No net
No easy bet
No let

Vision and vowels
Like following owls

No noose
Life is not caboose

Grinding and growling
Like old moose

Running with fray
Alone and gray

Never holiday
By the bay

In late May
Love takes away
Boulevard I stay

Making me pay
For another way

I stray
Like dead end sun ray

No Time

No time to write
No time for art

No time for love
Or looking above

The bard must have made time for his 38
When push came to shove

Stanza suffers
Syntax buffers
Release the snow white dove

Like ballroom banter
I tire of this bitter war

Haunted house without a door
Tank bought at the artillery store

I seek solace I will never find
A monk outdoors
Love unkind

On streets and interstates
No time for poetry

On alleys and avenues the full moon
Has apartment lips and candelabra hips

The window is broken
The muse is on the run

Broken crosses
Boardroom losses

Edging endless eclipse

Spirit of Saint Louis
Lost somewhere in rumble of rhyme
Gargantuan belly of crime

Avid anthems and arabesques
Midnight murders misbehaving mime

North Hollywood

Where the sun meets my moon
The friends I have
Are no friends at all

Begging for Hollywood's table
Like a loud crier

I love your narrow streets
And wide boulevards

The In N Out Hamburger
Of my heart

The lazy river that flows through
Your imagination
Like dust on a dollar

Is it all about you?
Does your day end in the mirror?

No Ho you have housed me for over 3000 days
And still you ask questions
A Messiah could not answer

A gaze into the future
A look at the past perhaps

But your Vinelands, Magnolias,
Republic of Pies and Raven Playhouses
Make up the Art's District
Where I live to walk

But does it all matter
When the sun sets?

And I am alone again
Mapping out this mine field

Not A Word

I called you this morning
Asking for help
Begging for an appointment
You never called back

For the first time ever
You showed a divine lack
While turning your back

You are abstract
Like a southern breeze
Blowing north

A sort of love aborted
Glue snorted
Disaster courted

But still
To leave me sitting in my shit
Without diapers

While you do nothing
But ignore me

I cannot fathom

Once we were friends
More even
Now we lick the equator
With a semblance of a reason

Not Enough

While I wash my hands
In the bathroom
Of the Starbucks
On Camarillo and Tujunga
In North Hollywood

I know the sin I commit
Cannot sit

I say I am doing fine
That lie of mine

The universe on my shoulders
Like ten ton boulders

I write and write
Seeking perfection
Leaking affection

Despising desecration
Embracing alienation

Palms clean
Thumbs stinking of spit

No one to blame
But the same

Playing this game
Not finding fame
Where is my name?
Lost in space
Without your face

Most beloved
Die for me

I leave this realm
With nothing to helm

Not your ocean blue eyes or

Somnambulant cries
The storm in my soul
Finds but dust and rust and
The kind of thrust
Only strippers know
When they sell what they must
For a ride on the pole

Please my love
Tell me what you need

How I bleed
On what complex you feed

For I know not
Of this lot

Where I belong
Who I am or

If coffee will kill
The cancer in my quill

PART II

PREVIEWING PURGATORY/
VOWELS AND VERSE
FROM THE STREETS TO KEATS

Now

6/16/15

Between life and if
Is everything but

A phrase bursting
Through the haze
In all its beige malaise

Stealing words
From some sort of phase
On this island of
Sheep that graze

Oves refusing to gaze
Perhaps tomorrow the puzzle will purify

Buying time
When time cannot be sold

Selling the sun
When the moon is full

Comets on parade
Like withered fins
Sinking beneath the din

Caressing demons
Polishing ovens
Ripping declarations

Peeling potatoes on the farm
With country charm
Like romance in the woods

Stars falling
Like an angry mauling

Oceans calling
Sand appalling
Wolves harming like insulated armies

Rivers flowing like jealous children
Babies crying like fallen apples

The staunchest arm
Yet to alarm

Numbers

1, 2, 3 and love I do not see
Through the prism of be
The very timeless see

I am drowning in RAM Storage and all those folders

I am cutting and pasting my poetry
Like a rock to a stone

My friends have abandoned me
My parents have died

And I sit with my wi-fi
At Starbucks knitting the future
Into the past
Like a forlorn poet lost in his dreams

Standing still is dying
Running is crying
Getting older is akin to trying

My Documents is full of My Desktop
Which relies too much on My Computer

Numbers make me feel alone
Like a park in a dumping zone

A theory without a supporting bone
A timeless lie at the foot of my soul
Can someone please make me whole?
Like the caterpillar who loves a mole

I lie in bed all day
Arithmetic makes it go away

Shoulders bleed from lack of use
Like fancy cars from land obtuse

My life needs to change
But numbers keep it on the same old track

Like Frank Sinatra without an ounce of lack

Obama

I voted for you in 2012
And I am glad

You pull the trigger Mr. President
Quicker than the liberals expect

You, the family man with the cool
Are no fool

When the Republicans
Block everything you do
You make policy as a moderate
Commander-in-Chief

You, the politician with sharp eye and honest ear
Are tethered to this earth

I do not agree with every call
From an unmolested hall
Buzzing like a mall
With an undefined pall

President Obama
You are taking us into the next
Two years with clarity and precision

But Isis and Syria, Iraq and delirium
Israel and Palestine
Ukraine not just in name
You are not quite on the dime

Keep on trucking
While the opposition dwells in the past
You build a bridge to the future

America
Open your eyes

Obama is a space shuttle
Headed for Hades

Officer of the Law

You did not arrest me
When I rode the metro
Without a ticket
While homeless

You pointed the way
To the outreach center instead

You were judge and referee
That hot September night on the Blue Line
Near Long Beach
Over eight years ago

Less judgmental than my parents
Quieter than my sister

You did not raise your voice
Or berate me like a child

You were at peace
At one with God

And I was not afraid when
I Stood up and proclaimed
"I have not paid the fare"

You listened more than spoke
Mr. Los Angeles County Sheriff's Department Officer
Prayed more than prosecuted

Open Minds

Belonging in the sun
Is the one
Who we all know
But do not

At the golf course a hole in one

Aces at the tennis court
Braces never at the dentist

Doctors are salesmen
Patients victims

He understands blood
Comprehends love

No hitters at the baseball diamond
Shutouts on the gridiron

Fists to the face at home
Children aborted
Abraham deported

Open Wound

Blistered biscuit
Ripped wrist
Sun slicing skin
Like sharpest fin

Torment tally
Poets rally
Alliteration alley
Instinct valley

Wounded bear
Clutching air
Lose to win
Next of Kin

Absurd family
Mediocre homily
Scissored vein

Tangled mane
Dripping with disdain
Tears falling like rain
On steepest pane
Battering driest plain

Oxygen and Water

11/21/14

Of what I know of air and H20
One covers me with you
The other with dew

Of what God tells me of
John and Judas
One served
The other got what he deserved

Of what I know of Christians
Many contradict the cross
The others mourn the loss

Of what I know of me and you
We will make it through
Like only do a few

Of what I know of politics and religion
One barricades the door
The other sits on the floor

Pappa Proud

When you shave that thick Czech face
In front of the mirror
In the bathroom attached
To the bedroom you do not share with your wife my mother
Because you are afraid you will disturb her at night with your work
I run into my mother's arms and
Tell her that you are wrong

She agrees but nothing changes
Nothing ever changes at
839 Roseland Parkway in Harahan, Louisiana outside New Orleans
Until I turn 23 and Jesus is juxtaposed
The jury jangled
Judas justified
The moat molested

Pappa your face saves me when reality and fantasy collide
In a maelstrom of trembling wrists and smothered gifts

Down at the five and dime I look for another set of nerves
Because the one I have has been splintered to smithereens
By a mental hospital with white coats, pink pills, thick walls and butchered lives

Patricia

The chipped teeth mark the hypotenuse of refrain

As the soft skin of you
Holds my cheeks aloft
Through yet another midnight

Please do not injure me with
That sharp tongue

Shards of me left on the milky
White ground

Smile feeds another
Wild laughter at Chinese
Food place
Dancing alone at Jack in the Box

Society runs you amuck
Like salt in shaker

My muse
My twilight wanderer

Sometimes you put brain in front of heart

I weep
Only to awake to orange dusk
In your eyes

Symphony of syllables
Swinging from your cylinder
Like pockmarked sky on strawberry lips

Patricia, My Lady

I found you when I was not looking
When the no's were so much
Louder than the yesses

You the tiny dancer with the
Voice of an eagle beckoning

You, my dearest, have more
Life than a comedian heckled
A bull ripping red

I see the world in those hazel headlights
That beaten down idealism
Crying for a reprieve from the storm

You laugh, my love, and the
World laughs with you
You are my iceberg thawing
My actress dancing Darwin

You kneel at midnight mass
The universe kneels with you
My bible girl in the middle of her own sugar swirl

You have made me a better person, I think,
With the drama and little girl blink

I now open my hand
And lead my own rock n' roll band
Drawn in the sand
Like a camel without a brand

Fumbling with fate Digging up dawn
Rediscovering dusk

I fear marriage again
The push and pull
The confusion and pain

But this time I will not stop
I will not be afraid

For suffering and healing are two
Sides of the same coin

I will climb the tallest of mountains
Like a hiker looking for the summit in the clear

Because of you I try
Because of you I do not lie
Because of you I will not die alone

Perhaps

I am here to prepare for there or
To take a break from there

It feels like here is a downhill ride from there
A cub from grizzly
A seed from Redwood

In the cycle of life
What comes around goes around

Dearest New York City
My lady of life
Beast of breath

Fool me not
Clear the path for my return
Third reincarnation
In your shadow

Your boroughs of banter
Get ready the deck

Allow the river to go
The moon to glow
The sweat to flow

Number three is the charm
Getting there is sounding the alarm

Petra

8/22/14

As the words leave your mouth
I am poisoned by the beauty
Of their song

The very awkward angle of their reach
The singular syntax of your skin
The sadness you harbor within
Whether wet or dry
Dead or alive
Jazz or jive

The language of you is the soul of you
Syllable and subject
Predicate and possibility
Adjective and adverb

I love you
The bible says to
I love you
My heart gushes with atrocious agony
And grungy galoshes

I love you
For I know nothing else
I love you
For you give when the world screams take
And the heavens cry do not make an artificial lake

Rain falls
You are not wet

Snow gathers
You stay warm

Only saints know your path dearest cousin

Philadelphia

Bucks County embraced me
Like coffee sugar
Like the kind of boy
Parents analyze
And friends understand

Mother and father tossing me into two mental hospitals

I no longer ask why only when
How not how come

Langhorne, my Langhorne
No friends
No ends
Up ended by time
Loosened by rhyme

Poetry an escape
Closed fists banging open
Mind dreaming

What do you want from me?
Love does not smother
Compassion finds another

Murder father's merry- go-round
Kill mother' s cannibal

City of brotherly love
You showed me vanilla
And fed me strawberry
Bathe me in snow

I walk Florida sand during Pennsylvania Winter
Like man expected to be boy and
Function like adult

Philly, my silly Lilly
Rain history on my scar
Like tar under my car
To end the war at even par

Pieces of Gold

After eight years
I am getting back the
Crossword puzzle of my heart

The jigsaw puzzle of my spirit
The very sense memory of the sun

I sit on Mount Aetna no longer
Contemplating conundrums

Crossing gazes with
Alternate mazes

No longer blacking out inside orange busses
Whose destination I do not know

And fighting off the advances of gay men
At five in the morning
On bus routes all over town

Skid row sucking me in
Like superman overdosing on kryptonite

Captain America fighting
Without his shield

The incredible hulk
In street clothes

I no longer feel
Compromised and victimized

My hands tremble less
My knees do not shake

And the difference between
Then and now is a little
Confidence either way

Pigeon Droppings

1/13/15

Door opens
Your face beams
Like a thousand lights

Door closes
Your face shines
Like ten thousand lights

Window opens
Your voice loud
As a thousand eagles

Window closes
Your voice clear
As ten thousand crystals

Closet opens
Your eyes bright
As a thousand tomorrows

Closet closes
Your eyes turquoise
As ten thousand oceans

Drawer opens
Your mind supple
As a thousand yearlings

Drawer closes
Your mind nimble
As ten thousand pigeons

Dresser opens
Your feet as quick
As a thousand gazelles

Dresser closes
Your feet as sure
As ten thousand elephants

Purse opens
Nerves as jagged
As a thousand razors

Purse closes
Nerves as steady
As ten thousand abused women believing in pure love

Plane on a Chain

7/17/15

The metal tube rises
As if on a string
It is now king

Modern technology
To you I sing

Like a screaming fling
Not knowing a thing

You scare me
Unhinge me at the root
So I will not shoot
Scoot
File suit

I am lark
Who sparks bark
On scattered mark

As child
I flew over ocean green
Like dream
Without seam and
No scream

An adult now
I fear the plow and
Unwilling how

Landing on mountains and hills of row
Scuttling the sow
I slowly die
Oh so high
While I fly

I will not cry
Sigh or lie
Eating a lemon pie
Owning the sky
Like a fly
That I should not be able to buy
For some guy with a tie
To it all I only ask why
While for this earth I vie

In the tributaries of my mind
The ones that pass for gold
I am stuck in the monsoon of memory

Tears flow like rainwater into the drain

My ego has a bloody stain
That not even I can explain

Everywhere I go I feel the pain
From the mangled mane

I cannot find love
I try to look above

But lately all that gets me is a dead dove

I am as hollow as a wheel
Eating steel
Refusing to kneel

The gods of rhyme
Gather steam
Robbing me of my dream

But in the end
The mirror knows the price
Of not looking twice

JJ-The difference between the tree and the plant, the now and the then. You are the love of my life, the end of the divide between Czechoslovakia and America.

Jennifer, the answer to the answers of time, the very swell that rides the storms of dissatisfaction like a tiger riding truth, a cheetah counting rhymes in air, a nocturnal nabob nattering nannies like Nubian narcissus negating north. Jennifer, I love you. I need you. I want you. I cannot make it without you. I will unblock my senses and ride my endings like death uncoiled, life unfurled, tenderness squared. I love you my J, because love has no equal, no jolly grays, no ruddy nows, no unholy theys, this is the beginning of the end of the middle, the kind of day that earns no night. This is the love that once had caskets oiled and marriages prolonged. The love I longed for like a cup thirsting for plastic, a cherry yearning for seed, a dead bullet seeking danger for the sake of an unfinished beer.

Jennifer, you in your benign orange, you Armenian Jew who cannot relax, who does not like the endings of fairytales unless they include her. The Armenian Jew who wants the kind of love only god can make, only Buddha can produce, the kind of living living was not made for, the only I in an Indian ocean of j's. Jennifer, you giving, biting, sorceress of rose negligee and tomato-colored eyes.

You, my lover, my maturing, mitigating reason for the rockets of time finding the underbelly of rhyme. You, my living, breathing vixen of dime, mistaking anger for thyme, once more finding the right a for the wrong b, once more the days turn to angry nights, finding the right angles of nuance to slow the steady roll of progress.

> Jennifer, you uncommon happy hirsute of hiccup hysteria, you now gaze at
> me as I slumber seeking revenge for twenty years of self-inflicted agony.
> Jennifer, storm my senses like winter uncoiled, like jam unjarred, the sky
> unturquoised, like soil darkened.

I once had you by the scruff of the hair, the unreal real. But I cannot get you, get you over there, get you over here, cannot find you, cannot really ever know you, cannot truly sink my soap into you. You, my refined refurbisher often think you are wrong when you are right. I need you now. I love your ankles like rainbows. I live to tell you the truth like the meadow does rain.

Invisible to Myself

The North Hollywood Red Line runs back and forth from the 7th Street Metro station all night, it seems, or at least it did last night.

3am found me head down arms sprawled on my seat. The older, bearded black man across from me had hardly moved for the last hour.

> I exchanged gaze with a larger transit officer through the window as I quickly
> sat up. This was my third straight night of riding LA's after prime-time follies,
> the tragedy without names or ratings. The self-esteem had taken a battering.
> I had a hard time looking at myself in the mirror. The officer acknowledged
> the inevitable. The growing chasm between the number of homeless and the
> city's ability to do anything about them.

I had never in my 42 years felt the disappointment and shame I did then. My parents' dreams for a happy and contented life for me seemed to have gone somewhere haywire since coming to Hollywood from Carson, CA with $50 in my hand.

> I had spent the last 20 years of my life acting, writing, telling jokes and singing. Now, my attempt at finally making money from what I loved had hit tinseltown's underbelly like a dead pigeon. The land of dreams had turned into the valley of demons, most of my own making.

I had left New York City a few weeks earlier to rid myself of the wannabes and you don't know until you tries that had haunted me for so long. This, my 24th trip to Los Angeles, would find me atop Laurel Canyon or just another carcass.

I knew down deep, however, that the city I so loved and admired had iron jaws this time around. On Tuesday, my fourth straight day of wandering, the whispers and frustrations of Angelinos would come full fore.

Exiting the Beverly/Vermont train station in dirty gray New York Rangers sweatshirt and bag a large Hispanic man selling wares launched into a long and passionate diatribe aimed at me.

I told him to "go fuck himself." This aimless roaming, this rousting about with the universe had changed me. It made me mean. Made me bitter. Made me need to stand-up for myself at every corner and declare that I am alive, I do matter, and I will never not make a difference.

> The two ladies near the bus stand on Vermont had the final word.
> "At least," the older one said to the younger, "he doesn't have to take off that shirt here."
> I felt like I was beginning to lose something much more precious than a shirt.
> If I hadn't lost it already.

Blue Eye Beautiful

There in the corner
In my corner
You always were
Something

Something with brains

Something with wings
With bling

You rose until
You fell

Like a great building
You just stood

Like a grand beating
You gave

Like my friend
You strayed

Like the end soon
You will not die

Not with those lungs
Not with those blue bright ones

Not with the fingers
Big brother

The ones that barely bend to break
We are brothers
From the same mother

Salty Syrup

Half of what I have you got
Half of what I need you decide
Half of what I provide you already have
Half of half is still not whole enough
Half of whole begs to differ

But half of you is not enough to satisfy most all of me
At least until the time you begin to believe.

The Dying is Easy here on Lankershim
The blinds get pulled
The teeth get sharpened
The fingers break
And the life gets taken
Sausage egg and cheese mcgriddles
Order 368

The Chain on the door

There on the knob
Near my throat I feel your love

The same love
That once found the
Bottom of my top

Now seems to have
Made the puddle
Smaller

Now seems to have
Made the dent so
Much taller

Radio Alive

Me on the floor
Next to my headshot
Like a careening car

The little black phone
Minds its mind
Like Judy Garland at MGM

This could work
This could take-off

This could could
If we gave it a chance

I put the radio on
After I finally
Realized I couldn't
Do it all alone

After yesterday
And today became one
In a haze of tomorrow

Citrus Angel

In this world of one
You were two

In this fragmented
Three

You were four

In this heartbreaking
Time-traveling ozone layer
You floated above

In this golden chalice
Of existence

You finally cut silver
Like a bad thief
Bettering

Mother #2

And she walks to walk even
Less some more

And she shakes in her face
When she listens to not listen

Like like like the ground
Shook when she first
Saw not me but the
Beige skin around my eyes

When I saw the cement
Fibers surrounding
Her skin

And the crescents
Around her hazel eyes

Seasons

Winter often calls my name
Summer rains
In buckets of three

But here on this green
Bench I see a
Chance for friends

Maybe autumn
Will soon find me

Living in the
Same street as you

Bellowing spring
The way you

Bellowed my noose

Valencia Gold

Yes there in that
Catholic school
I hated

You waited for me
Over in Europe
That same year

I accidently
Kicked you in the
Rear

I tried to apologize
But you hooked
Into your fears

I remember I didn't
See you for years.

Trampled In and Trampled On

She did it to me
I did it to her

But at least
In the end
My voice was
I think tighter

Was just lighter

After a thousand days and nights
I can barely find my sight

The old guitar stands in the corner

The middle of the day
Weighs heavy on my prey

As the buzzing phone
Majestically tatters dark

The pier in Malibu
Was missing the u

The Denny's
Was closing-up

And my wife and
I had chewed each
Other up

The plane in the
Sky was leaving
LA just like me

Basically Blurred

Maybe the days between our fall
Have been few

And the Indians in
Our past
Too many to mention

Maybe the path
Between what
Was and what
Might be was
No path at all

Maybe who we
Once were and
Who we wanted to be

Were one
And the same

But the hours between
Our rise will be few

And the distance between
Our days will be
New

Santa Monica

I sit overlooking
The beach in
Santa Monica

Over there in the
Corner they
Kiss like it really
Mattered

I turn away
Into the very day

Thinking to myself
If only love mattered

If only I weren't
So battered by myself

Then maybe, just maybe
The shore would save me

Manager Lady

Those wicked
Wicked eyes
Close like butterflies

My heart she sometimes clutches
My side she sometimes stitches

It is the sea
That often saves her

It is the sky
That never names her

It is her soul
That always blames her

Breakfast Buffet

Over here in the sand
The sun slides like you

Burying the things
That matter

Buying the avenues
That clatter

In the wicked
Pain I held
In my brain

You slammed
The door like God
Hardly mattered

Three-and-a-half Times at the Airport

Here in LA
Parking concourse 6
Sits opposite
Spirit Airlines

One Sunday morning
About three

I sat there
For eight hours
Waiting

The people passed
The luggage crashed

And one more time
She did not show-up

And one more time hope
Hit the wall

And one more time
Faith lost all

Wander

On the corner of
Slauson and Crenshaw
You just know

You just know that Jesus
Is a word for the next pancake breakfast
And your old
Socks belong rolled-up
Like that at the bus stop

The shelter
That ol'shelter
Was full last night
With all three white boys

Yeah, the Wing Works
Sat vacant
Next to Taco Bell
Saturday morning

And well,
I walked to get to
The next intersection

To that smiling young Spanish
Lady with the rolled-
Up hankie in her hands

And this is where you
Learn how to be
How to be before
Really, really living

How my sister turned
Me down for a hotel
Room on my fourth night
On the street

How I got-off the medication just to have it, well,
Get off me

And then I

Called you
Because I knew
You'd understand

Knew you'd not
Lie at least, I thought,
Until you had to

Thank god the subway
In LA doesn't have workers

Like when that guy stepped out of
Nowhere in his own drama
Near the tracks

And even I was scared

Rode up and down
All night and didn't realize
I smelled so bad people
Were avoiding me

The cops gave me
A ticket

And told me
They hope I'd
Make it to the
Out Reach center

That night
Earlier I made eye
Contact with the
Big fat transit cop

As he didn't board the train
At the metro station

And the 108 on the
Corner has three people
Waiting

The poets in New York
Keep waiting

And you told me
Yesterday you had
No romantic feelings left

And your sister
Sure does 'cept
Only her mirror knows

The cops here in
Madland need 25
Cars to make an
Arrest

Seems like two or three
Would be smarter and
I wait for you
Knowing you won't come

I'm tired of talking
About me

Little ol me ol' nothing me
Let's talk about you
And the big hole in your cheek

Your eyes
That avoided me in the
Mental hospital

Like you knew
If you looked
The truth

Would show itself

And then you
Would have to look your
Self in the eyes

And maybe tell the
Truth you'd not been tellin'
Because it hurt
Or it wasn't really
The truth or it got
Away too easy

Or bein' the head
Social worker
Had not been what you wanted anyway

And the anger will
Be free

And the reason you
And me and you
Is now one
Is not a reason
And an excuse
To stop looking
For answers that
Never come
And doors that never
Open and time that
Never stops and
Love that never breaks
And people that never mistake

Then the orange bus
Came and the folks
Got on board

And I was alone
At the bus stop

And the grandfather
And little boy
Crossed the street

And the shirt I bought
at Macy's in New York
is inside my Luggage
on the street

The morning is getting old
The lights are getting long
And the fever in

My soul is back again

I wonder when
The joke will be told

And if my name is something I hear between
Breaths and if the
Pink shirt I bought at Macy's
Is not some cheap
Artificial way to get
SoCal street cred
Like being white in
Black America

Little

The little library
Off Hauser looks new
And cement it is full
Of plastic tables with signs
That tell you not to bring
Food or drink

The whole place is wooden
And metal and white and Japanese
And black and maybe tennis shoes
And glasses

The sidewalk around here is pretty clean and the apartment buildings are
Yellow and canary yellow
And they kind of jump on
Each other like building blocks
Or ice cream or the capital letters
On the side of a big truck
And the watches meld to
Loudness mold to information signs
And the bold blonde hair on my
Nephew is too damn white like an
Old man painted staccato
Near the window of his downtown
Apartment old train going by outside

It is the whiteness
The balls, the looping eyebrows
That already make me think
I can be better
I can climb steps
I can fix houses
I can lift toilets
I can walk into
The middle of the street and stop traffic
I can look at my thumb and dance
To Gershwin in an Isley Brothers sort of way
I can walk down movie house aisles
In socks and bare feet and
Look like a husband and father and
Hallways in houses that curve

If you want them to like steaks
On a barbecue
I can nosedive
Into space nothing black
I can close one eye a dolphin
And hold one hand a child
While smiling face
Pulling lips tight I can grip the pen and
Touch the paper with five fingers on my
Left hand
The tips feeling the up
The Seroquel levels off in a lot
Of pain and doubt and
The kind of needle that
Lets you know that\
Without a stomach there wouldn't be
Suicide or hara-kiri or
Vietnamese concentration camps or big boats with lots of
Chains and people and oars and
The down is as quick as the up and
I forget and I shake and the ribs

Come together like sandwiches and
The forehead straightens and the fingers lineup like frozen sausage strips
In an open freezer at the supermarket and the neck and throat
Are one like an island in the middle of the top of the body
The chick over there is asking me to do too much and we haven't talked.

I called her because I loved her
Not for me
Not for us
For nothing
For time

The motel on Sunset
Sits quiet tonight
The cars go by like
So much rain

And I ain't got nobody
Finally I ain't
Got nobody
Nobody to massacre
Nobody to tow
Nobody to tolerate
Nobody to owe
Nobody to disagree
Nobody to flow
Nobody to indemnify
Nobody to know

Dead and Homeless Again

Room 204
Bleeds Czech
Vomit

The door is too
Damn white

The carpet too damn gray

The shu don't bite

The fucking electric chord has
A mental history
And I can't live not like this anymore

But the words come
They come like dandruff
They come like snow

And Sunset comes too
Not the street though

LA Again

Leonard Bernstein looked happy
Oh, Leonard Bernstein

I left downtown tonight
Left the shelters
Left the trains
Shit, I left my brains

Vermont never ends

Broadway this Broadway anyway
Is colder than my head
And deader than Broadway

Music

I once ran track
Music is track
Without the shoes

It is oh God
Yes it is

It is not

When it is not

I know it should be

I know I miss
It like my mother's hand

I need it like skin
I want it like tears

I demand it like
Love
Which cannot be demanded
Can it?

They say I should write

Write
Write
Write they say

But I cannot
I can't

I am performer
Too

Sun raiser
Leg churner
Face giver

Never enough
But always there like my father

The writing
The words
The performing on paper

And tomorrow morning
I go again into the street

Into garbage
Into my heaven

Soldiers

They walk the
Streets in
Crutches and pain

In bandages and shame

Over there under
The palms of LA
They lay

Not giving blame

Soldiers of themselves

Soldiers of the game

Soldiers they spit
Soldiers they tame

Soldiers die young
Soldiers, oh, soldiers same

Disgusting Deadly Sex

God, I hate
The science of sex

I've never done it

It's too much for the woman
Too much up and down

Too much the same
Old chaps

Too much an act
Not a love

Too much this
Too much that

Not enough this

Not enough that

Fucking is about as
Creative as jello

As selfish as pain

Trampled in and Trampled On

She did it to me
I did it to her

But at least
In the end
My voice was
I think tighter

Was just lighter

After a thousand days and nights
I can barely find my sight

The old guitar stands in the corner

The middle of the day
Weighs heavy on my prey

As the buzzing phone
Majestically tatters dark

The pier in Malibu
Was missing the u

The Denny's
Was closing-up

And my wife and
I had chewed each
Other up

The plane in the
Sky was leaving
LA just like me

Adam suddenly realized he was alone. He had left his wife Swan a month ago. He had no money, no apartment, no car, and he had forgotten where he put his luggage.

Adam felt the tingling in his feet. He felt the electricity push him out the door. He wanted to be near someone, anyone. He just wanted to be touched lovingly, kindly with some kind of affection. He just wanted to talk, to Swan, to anyone.

Adam quickly walked outside. He walked by glass doors, he walked by one-wheeled bicycles, he walked by people standing, he walked by people talking, he walked by people sitting, he walked by people laughing.

He found himself crossing a huge cement chunk of road, a sort of street extension. He saw the "Don't cross" sign.

He couldn't live like this anymore. He wanted to be understood for his talent. He wanted some measure of success, some respect for his abilities, some peace of mind, a family that allowed him to be himself without threats or judgments, a wife and children that would accept him for who he was not for who they wanted him to be.

Adam let the airport police stop him.

The two officers in dark blue slipped cuffs around his wrists. The one on the right asked him if he was on medication.

Adam told them he had been on and off the meds.

He wanted a couple of weeks of free room and board. Some time just to get away and think. Some time to stop thinking about Hollywood, money, family, God, Bush, mother and changing the world as an artist.

As the police car pulled into Harborside/UCLA Psych. Ward the blindness had disappeared. The truth of his stomach, his beautiful goddamn, Czech stomach lay bare for the gorgeous shrink to consider.

> "I want my Swan," he said. "I want the soft, soft, tender touch only a woman can give. I want to find some peace and tranquility. I lost my mother five years ago," he said, "and I now left my Swan my love. I can't stand it. I want to have a nervous breakdown in the middle of Sunset Boulevard. I want to fail. I want to be a lunatic, I want to want to be insane like a mute."

She, in polite smile turning grim, listened and put hand on his.

In 20 years of psychiatric care, that had never happened. And he knew he was alright and he knew everything would be fine. And he walked into the glass enclosed observation room and stopped. Surrounded by sleeping lunatics, all in their white underwear and dead faces, he for a moment considered where he was.

"I want to play music," he yelled. "I want to sing, I want to be the best lead singer in history. Forget Mick Jagger, forget Axel Rose. I am the beginning without end."

And the orderlies in blue surgery gear did not stop him. They did not tell him to shut-up. No, they stood and they watched and they understood. They kind of smiled actually. They also admired it.

And he spent 17 days at Del Amo.

And he met his Yvette in the best two days of his life. And they shared a forbidden romance in the nut house.

And then he was sent to some independent living facility where the bodies hung low, the fear invaded like a panzer tank and Mrs. Pike, the Chinese owner, milked money from the mental patients like crab cakes at an Ohio bake fest.

And after she tried to get $300 more out of him that he didn't have, he left a note and took off for Hollywood with his last $50.

Somewhere inside this hollow dome he called his brain, he must have made the decision to be homeless rather than in a mental facility. He would rather spend time with honest lunatics than put upon ones.

But before giving into this grimmest of reapers, he tried for his late mother's sake, to get free medication from his Medicare Part A card.

The Chinese pharmacist's hands at the Sav-On on Vermont Avenue shook as he, one of at least five in L.A. told him the Seroquel would cost $40 as part of his co-pay, and he could not give it to him as a part of his health insurance.

"Even if I really, really need it," he asked the pharmacist. The pharmacist said nothing. The next morning in the bathroom of the McDonalds on Sunset and Crescent Heights, while expecting the police to burst in, he flushed all of the medication. He decided on survival over sanity.

The next week he slept in trains, bus stops, busses and benches. He traveled L.A.'s vast bus system with an expired bus pass. He was issued a ticket by sheriff's deputies at the Compton Blue line stop while sitting in a dirty gray New York Ranger's sweatshirt unshaven and unshowered with a huge torn plastic bag carrying valuables in his lap. People around him were pointing and whispering.

Some were holding their noses and turning-away as he opened the bag.

He spent four nights in shelters in LA's skid row where the roaches and rats often do a dance of love amid the teeming piles of garbage. Walking down Slauson to San Pedro every night to the People Helping People shelter was akin to being the last man standing in an atomic bomb blast. He wondered how these special people could find depth, warmth and a cup of Lipton in this almost nether-reality.

Thursday night he arrived at People Helping People at 8PM. He was turned away.

"Full," he was told. "I'll take a pew, a cot, a piece of floor," he said.

"We're full-up," the shelter manager said sitting at his desk reading the newspaper. He nodded to his second-in-command, a balsy, head-tottering security guard without sharing eye contact.

"Come on, man," the security guard said, "you know how it goes."

"I appreciate what you all have done for me," he said, "but you could have taken me in tonight." The next day amid a mid Saturday's busy afternoon traffic, the public phone on Sunset and La Brea cascaded with tall Czech artist slamming phone against metal box.

"Send me the money," he screamed at his father on the other end outside Philadelphia. "I don't want to spend another night on the streets."

A couple of hours later, he picked-up $750.00 at the Western Union on Sunset and Wilcox. After a week at the mid-Hollywood Hilton located at the Mark Twain Hotel on Wilcox, Lankershim Boulevard found a new dweller, this time a fresh-faced Czech lad near the NoHo arts district with much to prove and much already proven.

The bearded man sitting next to me has eyes like rockets and lips like rain. He sashays in his seat like oil at breakfast and stares at the magazine in his hands like a beaver at broken wood. The white hair on his chin seems to say he once tried but could not find his reason, his way. The path took him to the end where devils play and the avenues of hope criss-cross like bargains at a matinee, like pieces of time avoided. And I think of my life and its uneven consequences, its crooked line, the chalk mark offended by listless action, by tomato time, by the kind of ignorance reserved for lighthouses and chimneys, the barking of voices, the caressing of beach towels.

The sensation he gives of hands on tray table reminds of the anger of silence, the wisdom of horses, the bruised hips of risk, the white salt of tears dripping towards absolute annihilation, towards notices dropped like bumblebees and ambitions misplaced like cold hard truth.

The man sits smiling often at his wife in a kind of yes, he is alive, he belongs, he cracks like sleeping plaster, he gets what he needs through what he wants. He is master of himself therefore everyone else. The things that are bad about him ultimately make him good. He makes so much sense sense no longer applies. He sees children stealing dreams they never earned and people laughing at concepts they never learned, he sees the good forgotten, the angry blamed and the lovers envied, he knows the time is nearing and the smoke is billowing, the leaves are falling and the bruised hearts are not mending, he contemplates suicide but thinks the better, he contemplates revenge but the light turns red, he limps like a bare-chested hater, but corrupts like an avid skater, his vowels have consonants, his angels horns, his diaries in black ink carry like the fog, he dances to the trouble truth once foretold, he is the nation of countries, he is the battered lamb, he does not follow his instincts, he crows the common land, he massacres again and again only to the hand, showing dentists the lingering long bang, he sings of battered fingers belonging to battered hands, he does not audition, he does not really know how, he lands in foreign prisons in the cavity of his mind, he blisters pronouns with the sanity of his hand, he is afraid of touching the wrong actor on the wrong hand, he needs 80,000 not 80 for his band, he tries and tries to forget the past and all its seeds, he needs so very desperately a love that does not see, a very uncommon and godly river without bending tree. He asks for hands cupped like pythons, the very woman he saw in his mother's womb, the tenderest touches, the most gentle giving stare, there you are and there you sit fish tank at the rear, hands bending at the hip, knuckles touching glass.

Only in story books of Cleopatra and Helen of Troy has he sensed a power so unrehearsed, a train station without rails, an attorney holding Jeremiah part II, she the one with glory does not feed the flock, she like he confesses at the altar of the cross, sitting below Jesus like eagles in the roost. She comes, one she, like a lassoed cloud, a heavenly poem metaphors and midgets milking

Mao, perhaps the phosphorescence of then like a grand piano unturned finding form, acknowledging rape, arguing assonance, maybe the piano is no pirate, it is but wood without skin, wheels on artificial ambulance, once amber, now orange, once polite, now real.

The face of her skips circles in ice, pirouetting past progress, now pandering joy, but never, lo never, exacting excuses for partying prison without bars or oars without leads or beads without death or BET, but always, lo always, with the kind of breath that raises universes and invites philosophies. Always her face, that brunette cark lace of Indian ice, that incandescent yes to the world's no, that unremarkable maybe, that yard sale tie born aristocrat azure. She is the heavens, of the many hands that shake blue, of the enormous gap she has yet to find, will never find, can never find, does not know how to find. She loves to swim in grass, dig in bass, and sing to mass, but she does not like to, well, be rescued. I am rescuing her from being rescued, walking the living wonder, faking the draw play around center, and perhaps, if so lucky, seeing the doubt in her hazel headlights, her stained glass. There in the weakness of strength, the past leaning on tomorrow, the brazen tom foolery of kids, I lay dreaming of just once hiding her near. Just once needing her swim, just once letting her go, just once lip on knuckle, just twice her body lingering for three touches, then four, perhaps as many as one more.

Below the kind of soul that mends pianos, the kind of black boredom born in cellars and alleys, live the elbows of our parents, the gashes of hate, the torn tissues of tendons that do not mend, the screaming of dead puppies, the cascading of modern dancers to music from other rooms, to petals from foreign flowers, to malleable massacres gone unnoticed because even they do not fit the thirst of waste or the fragment of taste, but they like wild mushrooms sap the wind of unnatural ruins, the guilt that daddy knew, the anxious anger of blackened billows, and yet the kind of torture never met the crime. Instead the wild petunias that billowed like mother's darlings now lead a double life. One contesting rhythm, the other love. Bells once tolled for glory, now for pain, for need, for genius, the kind of feeling machetes fear and messiahs inebriate. God's first child has but one name, Linda. The black hair, the soft neck, the bent Kim Novak eyes, the straight lips, the untaken gaze, own this universe. The blazing cheekbones, the untitled spirit. The bells ring like chimes on a silent echo, never sensing the rhythm cascading too far away from elms and burdened horses. Nor do they answer to yesterday's forests and the hills and mountains of lament. The honest love is never the realest, but the shallowest at once showing purity and at best killing the fear of that doubt. The hands holding each as if the sea mattered, as if yesterday has no name, as if love was but a memory, one few remember, but all know.

The red door of room 220 seems confident, but inside sits a man of little malfunction whose main duty is passion, is love, in intelligence. For they are the branches that guide the universe on the gentle shastas it forgets like slippers at a ball. There in the near distance lay the ricochets of war. His mind flattened by scenarios of airports and bathrooms, the kind never entered only by the ruminations of quiet longings and vistas long forgotten by his ribald memory, his once-chaste mind.

And often he runs like a gazelle only to walk like rain across the forehead. He gallops the beige desert and yearns for the kind of love he knows, the desperate but true vision of memories remembered and sidewalks renamed. Only the i's are dotted and the t's crossed, only his like needs saving.

And the hardest lesson is the humility of hosts, the unflinchable telling of the truth to the silence of ears, the deflating of egos, the jealousy of laughter once distinguished now screaming like concrete calloused.

Things happen for a reason. But the reasons are water, flowing through palms like aspirin, then perhaps begging for thunder in a maelstrom of pancakes. This fiction, this love of his life, this stuffing what we feel, this aborting what we know, this stifling the avalanche to feed the worms below, to sting the manatee that once molested girls, that once even mattered a little because they prayed to metal. And the newspapers that shred genius because it has no deadline, no form, no goddamn structure, no enforceable nature, the journalists who abort for fame, greed, success and money. Where is the love of truth? Where is the professor with long hair talking about integrity and dignity.

"I never let facts get in the way of a good story." That from a famous sports columnist New Orleans way. And which he will of course deny.

You cannot stop a river or bend a forest. You cannot deny the attraction. Or carnage will follow. We will marry. We will love truly and deeply. We will dot each other's t's and cross each other's i's. This love, this cutoff donut in stomach, will sky and rain, pollute the darkness of doubt, the wetness of jazz, the ambivalence of criticism, the joy of absolutely nothing then something, the shores of pages that not one human reads, but everybody needs. The emptiness of lighthouses at midnight, the crawling, giving, scrolling of suicide, the fawning, tasting know know know of falling elephants. The given politeness of plants. The unforgiven sadness of love, but not with her as my rough long fingers flow through her dark brown hair, as the mast that once sailed free now sails not at all. As words mean little and actions spell truth divine. As I know it will be there when I need it. As the protected call for approach and the wicked for appeasement. I must watch laziness and lust and fame and success. They can corrupt the truth of me.

I almost get lost in the scenarios. And found my way to the ground, to reality. Los Angeles is a man eater. I smell carcasses in the corners. It leans on money. Boys and girls on drugs, alcohol or medication. God is dead. Or at least at Martha Plimpton's house for early brunch. And I need a publisher. I need love. Love is the foundation. I demand true, fire love, the kind that accepts blindly and judges not at all, the kind I have never had. The opening of doors once locked before breakfast. The giving of hearts better left taken. There in the corner behind the inner tube, behind the mask that is my face is the last instance of love revealed and lost, love nestled between two avenues, love molested in time, often submerged beyond recognition, but never given to tender animosities between sheets of graying red. Between snows of apple green, around thorns of endless pining, there in the naked clearing that once ended on Main Street, but now continues onto Maple.

In the last appraisal, love looks worn by nine maybe ten, but often collapses at twelve as the sky touches torches not made for seconds or minutes. Bad love is not love at all. It kills. Sex Kills. The Beatles were not right. Spoiled love can knock you to shreds. It can help you locate the lost child in yourself, the angry dresser, the manipulated boy scout, the incarcerated mud of languid lives lost in balanced manipulation. Then Linda came, light of lights, the anger of bastioned childhood, the tumultuous thunder of tomorrow's bathroom menu. The silence. The breathing of elves waiting for scraps their masters could not find. The love she has brought imploding inside my skull like tic tacs of tender origin. I cannot give-up on my art so quickly. I cannot lend the world spoiled milk. The Glendale phone call: minutes of wild tenderness chest over waist over white concrete over heaving madness once removed never replaced. There over there the carnage continues as saddle-backed donkeys lose the passion that once moved. The medication kills by numbing numbing the number.

And the fantasy is better than the reality until they meet. Until they marry, until the be is stronger than the are, until the is maneuvers past the frantic are of windowless nights and partied possums like a chagrined tastemaker from the coast of borderless clouds. By the second trip to LA the friends had gone and only the stench of her perfume up in room 312 of the Jeeves Hotel in Beverly Hills mattered, the thin arms that made me, the large tits that forbade me. I got more that night than ever before. It was naked giving, spontaneous love, affection, the kind that changes lives and thoroughly upends reality. This was a mirage wasn't it? A moment of reality magnified? No, this was real never to be forgotten. This stomach-to-stomach hand rubbing tight middle will forever die to live. Outside, the turquoise lights of workdom shone in spells of antiquated freedom and dire anticipation for a world imagined only through my idealism and imagination like manna in a storm of gumbo.

A river can be damned, but a soul cannot. No matter the cost, love will see the dawn, love will eschew the demons, love will find its god. And I don't care what they say, strength lies in the margins, in the unrealized realized, in the muddy rivers that flow at once shallow, at once full, in the belly of mediocrity. And love is music, transcending race, religion, hate, jealousy, superficiality and death. At my funeral I will rise to What's Goin' On and fall to Crocodile Rock. The path may fork, but it will come back. It may fall and it may rise, but it will bend. Spirits never die, they splinter. Happiness is not forgotten, it lives on in wiser days. The love she and I share has no moments or apostrophes, it is, it grows, it behaves as it will. It minds the store of change with unerring kindness and mutual admiration. And the Catholics forgive. They are not brick and mortar. They, behind curtains of gold and black, meet God and tether rope to your soul, embrace the good in your bad and forgive. The idea is to live like Jesus, to help the poor, the indigent and the blind. To be a man for others, to think of others as much as yourself. To let love lead, forgiveness follow and peace conclude. Gain strength from those behind shopping carts, lying in gutters and wrapped in blankets on snowy New York nights. I became one twenty years ago. No, I wanted help. As with my mother, I fell into their vice grip. I helped them instead of sharing my real gifts. I imagined my gift to be about them. Instead, it was about me, but I used them to cap the void, to give me an excuse for not dealing with the fame, success and responsibility of history. The Beatles are not just a band. The Rolling Stones are just a band. They made themselves matter. By standing for something bigger than themselves, something that helps ordinary people. Something that gives them hope, gives them a reason to look forward to tomorrow. Something my father understood and his father. Something Americans often forget. Something patriotism here forgets. Something called love of country, love of duty and love of freedom.

The night was not black, it was original. The two stayed in opposing rooms on that third floor that night.

After dinner at a Hollywood diner they ended-up together in room 312. He a shell of himself sitting quietly in the corner of the double bed. She kneeling on the floor, dead face in his hands. Soon his hands were on her face, left palm touching the middle of her back. She light as light, blonde hair glowing in the early morning light.

Two wrap around each other like otters, his hands in her face. Her hands in his hair. The room was still. The chair was there. The two lay front to front in moments of beating silence.

> Morning would catch them different. The air soaked in the blood of the rest
> of their lives. If the end begins before the beginning, perhaps the love we
> share will never die.

Perhaps the end we begin will always be shy. Perhaps the knuckles of freedom are bruised for a reason. The flesh is no longer the soul. It is upon reflection the vessel. Soul and love seem the same, but need the vessel to part. So do you and I need each other to breathe. Need each other to shine. We will never know ourselves without knowing each other. We will never walk unless we run.

The eagle's nest seeks the once-bitten memories surrounded by eager alleys and benign tomorrows as the town that once did now bends participles like torn taters and the last name that once stood late now stands afternoon, the bent angles sipping nouns now devoted to yesterday's spangles and live pastures and tomorrow's frozen midas-mixers. The wet one believes the dry answers as they pass the mornings of plastic. The wooden desks take the splinters now devoted to air balloons. The children swing the little devils as the sky wraps tomatoes to toothpaste in the cauliflower breath of vagabond presidents sipping the once-forgotten sink. The water around the white cement often flows through the silicone sandwich paralyzed by the incumbent vanilla of tangent ice creams not yet catered for the smitten crew. The battered man in the shadows now owns the anticipated overflow of undignified angels splattering the pigment along the alleys and pastures of sonorous somnambulance and pre-tested tolerance. In the only heart that matters you tumble the gray cloud blue, you singe the red sky new, you blaze the white star glue down to the paralyzed nub of town. You once blew the lanes toward paradise into Ralph's and the potato crisis of tangent dreams torn by the cylinder of tormented smiles once given to drastic candles tempted by dreams of animated sailors finalizing garbage details prepared by nascent marauders who eat their young, who get from me what they cannot from others. Sometimes they touch me just to make sure they still can. Always they are man-eaters disguised as love-eaters. And the tigers come in pairs at the jungle. They resemble manatee at the shore. They live only at the corners and spill donuts in twos. At the green light, progress and apathy dance like sharks at a bar mitzvah. The terminal dark and distraught in this tunnel of gray, this bipolar wind machine, this mule of no burden, this rock and roll igloo without ice. Once the present mutilates the present, only the past can reclaim its place.

Standing at the funeral, the red orchid falls from her lapel and stands on its rear, a truncated soul, a bottomless pit of leather and lace. In the back by the pool table time corrupts the one reason death dances naked across the dance floor: dawn dealing crap at the five and dime. The web there is thicker than the web here. Webs exist not, but love, but different souls, but indifferent difference and she does not stop and she does not want to and her eyes are brighter when not seen and darker when visited and and and we do not see when we are alive. We but witness and see. We live the lights. We turn-off the focus in our heads and the organization in our loins. We barely lick the divide between us and us, I and me, we and we before the season ends and the back of our backs no longer matter. We lie on beds of grass, on fawns of lean, on Jesus by the river mean and then we disconnect like bulbs without, like ticks despise and bouncers realize over by the Seattle mud, the Northwest now and the credit card finds funds and the street lies like naked dust like harassed must perhaps denied crust and then there is her and her and her just that no less no more a fish in water. In the end there is the day without night, love without lust and the binding that goes in-between, there is the bluish red and the impishness of being. The scenarios come and go, the rock star president, the escaping hero of a lead singer, the family get-together rock show, and then there is me, the crazy t-shirt guy, the insane lunatic of a plane traveler, the stupid stupid idiot of a human being, the get-it-together son, and I better just get it together quick before I die.

The End of The Beginning-Half a Life's Story in three pages. I promise this to be merely three pages long in order to satisfy both the nay-sayers and the anti-Nixonites. Today is the first Thanksgiving I spend alone. 42 of them and this Czech lad-beast finally gets it. "American woman stay away from me," "American woman MAMA let me be" – Guess Who, 1973. "American woman, mamma you set me free." – Radomir Luza, 2006.

> Today at the hospital some nurse told me there is no place for artists. Interesting. Yes. True. Out-of-this-world crazy and broadly negative given the amount of young, middle-aged and elderly artists I have met. Maybe the time is now for this country to stand up for its creative souls, its rude, over-populated islands of artistic toil that often go not merely unnoticed, but unappreciated for decades upon end. Yes, the true, real artist does it for the gist, for the love of the craft, the art, the real thrill of doing, the anti-Christ of death.

I am tired of this art thing. Immediately and unobtrusively. I want out. But art is everywhere and everything. It sings Dinah Shore, it collapses bridges built by Gods. It merely is. It merely cannot be. Once in a while some great spirit comes along who breaks the back of the oppressors and bludgeons the workers at the same time. A jolly unstable poet willing to say what needs to be said. I am that soul. That surfer dude.

> Today all the ruckus about Michael Richards on the Sunset Strip broke-out like cheese on a pizza. Ultimately, the comedian is a lost artist. I cannot get enough. It requires great courage and impeccable timing. Every night can be tonight. Every three Comedy Store minutes can be a knee-jerk reaction to hosanna, a wonderful, trying trip to the timeless wonder of improvisation and courage, the ultimate task in public and self-service. Maybe the day will come when these starving, psychotic loners and losers will once more get the credit for their art.

Which it definitely and uncompromisingly is, from John Belushi's bloated corpse to Whoopi Goldberg's obviously in-your-face attack on white American uber-culture or the forging of the American Caucasian. In the end, it is the mulla that counts, if anything does. It is the freedom of the thing. To eat when you eat and drink when you drink.

This LA, this Los Angeles of my second life, often bleakens me, never entertains me and forever changes my focus on this life thing. This city is the deadest, most desperate set of blue eyes I have never seen. It collapses around the setting of plates at the table of one. It often narrows the marrow in my veins. It listens to the George Clooney of our time. The rest of them are all nuts. There is no Hollywood, no unobtrusive me, no flying nun, no screen test, no bipolar, no dignified way-out but suicide, it seems. I do not take to the high-fliers of society, the lesser-known trapeze artists of temerity, all feather and stock and no first-class ticket to the soul.

My family emerged from the cocoon of war like brazen monkeys from some overblown zeppelin. They marched through the isolation of Hitler and the dead forest of Russian rule like some punch-drunk ballerina looking for heroine on the streets of Bed-Stuy, on the avenues of North Hollywood. I often search my father's closet for some sign of achievement, some kind of intense stigma that yes he, the priest of partisanship, did indeed have an ego. He fails me always and never speaks of what he saw.

I am different. I saw shelters of brazen cement, sidewalks of bronze, the intense way men held onto their past even when it made little sense. I saw death in the eyes of many, turbulence in the jaws of few and the rotors of corpulence and timid acceptance in the jaded molecules of the many, head on cement like fallen tomato, body to follow. It was the unnatural pull of corporate America and Hollywood helium that once-and-for-all castrated the American film, the graceful peacock we all knew had a chance given the right worms and strings. It was there the Democrats lost and the Republicans gained. I saw not one shelter-dweller use a piece of his check for anything but drugs and alcohol. A crack pipe, it seemed, showed-up at almost every corner. It seemed in this subdued darkness that nothing worked, nothing wanted to work. The stench of failure was as real as rain, as foreboding as anger and as hollow as our uncle's old windpipe. You just made-it-through and wondered how the others did. It was in this jungle of closet kings and windmill teens that everything was made clear. The poverty, the unquenchable thirst for suicide and drug death among alcohol-ridden angst lickers and police-dominated gangsters, ended here where it began. Presidents may come and go, speeches may fall flatter than skirts at a lesbian ho-down, but the creaking bathrooms and subterranean tunnels of graffiti and self-abuse cannot seek the same fate. It is the heart, the soul that must be changed, subdued, somehow misdirected. Programs, food stamps and liberal paper towels cannot and will not make the difference. What will is not clear. It seems drowning in this sea of black doom is not an answer. Sports are a band-aid. When battered on all sides by negativity and dubious sarcasm the soul suffers an untenable death, left black and blue and hidden in the corners of time like a swan out of place.

Journey continued. It began and ended with the fair lass Linda. And on this night I feel like dying, feel like I will, I think of her, beautiful and bold, yet unable to live by herself or with anyone else, big, and bigger than life, easy to talk to yet not easy to understand. Her largest gesture, throwing her wonderful, beautiful collections of poetry into the garbage because the poetry scene in New York had not treated me well. And then the bar fight where I defended her honor while being shoved out the door. Why did it all seem so corrupt? Was I addicted to her? Did God have some larger purpose for me? My paranoia grows. The addiction grows. I am frightened for my life. I am frightened for anyone who gets in my way. There doesn't seem to be a way to go back, to return. The souls here in Los Angeles are black and cold and lonely. I am becoming one of them. I cannot find a way to grip reality. I am slowly losing touch with the world, it seems, becoming one of them. I want to write, write and only write, but it is frightening, it grows in ardor and pain. It cannot and should not be counted-out. Right now, it is all I have. I want a woman's tenderness, her sensitivity in the worst way. I am thinking of calling a prostitution service. My father seems unhappy with me. No one knows anything. This lost street of dreams, this unsteady maven of witches and warlocks is now my only avenue to some sort of peace and warmth. I cannot do this by myself. I cannot die. I will not die. I will do whatever it takes to survive, to create, to make my music. And it feels like the air has been let out of my balloon. The last two years have been good it, seems. They have allowed me to speak my mind and say what I feel. I no longer try to hold things in. I no longer take verbal abuse from people. I feel homeless in my apartment. I keep looking for excuses to make it to the next day. This has been a lost journey, a misbegotten turn towards grace. The last two years have been better than the four before. They have rendered me hopeful and real. They have shown me God willful and mean. Truly, God can sometimes look like the devil, but that does not mean he is not present. This was never truer than sitting on a bus bench at 3am aware of separate realities, two planes of existence battling for supremacy. God will win. God always does I think. But in the battle I may lose the very soul I have so long and hard fought for. I am more nimble, more elegant, more acutely aware of death and life than at any other time in my life. I will stay in Los Angeles as I always knew I would. This lost soul has found redemption in California, in the blessed but unangular marriage of commerce and art, of the timid tango that is not my life. Of the art, which is infused with spirit. They may think me this or that, but I tell you, I know who I am and what I can do. I have done more in three months in LA than three years in New York. Sometimes success can look a lot like failure. I am out here alone. No little ol' lady to cut and shampoo my troubles, my suddenly sordid life. No, I am where I was 20 years ago. I am naked and free. Truthfully, LA saved this boy. New York can hold on to its elitist ways. I saw no lights there. No dreams in the making. The lasting image of Linda is her standing on stage at the Cornelia Street Café one Friday at 6pm and, shackled by fear, reading some of the best and brightest verse I have ever heard. My work will undeniably be touched by her for the rest of my life. Such was and is her truth. Under your battered overpasses and yellow oceans, City of Angels, my autumn stretches wider than the Sahara and my winter shines brighter than the moon at midnight.

Poised to Bend

Mama's hands
Warm and forgiving
Brown as rain
Soft as mane

Comprehending the living
Sewing blanket of peace

Building army of understanding
Drunk on fleece

Days are shorter with
You wrapped around me

Friction on the fraction
Devotion with no lotion

Mama
Veins running through the pair

Light as air
Without a care

The dove in your hair
Calmly stares

While your hands
Ever fair
Stand at heaven's gate
Oh so bare

Porno Mourno

Published in February, 2015 edition of online literary magazine KYSO Flash   12/10/14

The flickering begins at 7:43 in the morning
Touching retina then soul by 7:44
Black background turning flesh orange
And alphabet blue

Confidence burning browser
Like tiger turning time
Heart pounding jackhammer
Legs twitching tambourines

Religion losing its place
Like orphan in bread line

Brain attacked
By boredom

No more numbers
No more letters

Just me and you
Conjoining in the clouds

Prius

Hanging by the very beak of business
The untroubled troubles
The galvanized gang of goons
Is my Toyota Prius
As sensitive as my stomach
As intimate as this poem

I drive all over Los Angeles
With my blood red beauty
My New England red bombshell

The beach sucks her in
Downtown towers
Hollywood shocks and shakes
Pasadena paws and purrs

She is human, I swear
My little predicate
My uncommon clause
In her own phrase

Sturdy and bold she is
Like a small Mercedes
Fitting into every parking spot
And all freeway lanes
Like a child waiting for Santa Claus
Or teddy bear come to life

My Prius is like a lollipop
She does not bite
The sweet candy of wheel world
And delivers the ride of the century

My humble
Yet horribly handsome
Barcelona red lover

Radomir

8/22/14

Resistance fighter's shoes slipped in rear of closet

Now you start anew

Except you cannot
You will

Politics or professor
You choose the latter

Awards stacked into back of drawer

We not me
America not found yet

Injuring son with European
Perfectionism and discipline
Like Molotov cocktail in face

Washing and drying Czech flag
Even you know not what to do with old guard

Progressive genius on the brink
But Communist death list made you blink

Escaping to America made you blue
But not like son you thought you knew

Whom you gave your name and that awesome game

Now he searches for a modicum of fame
To make up for the sum of maim

Radomir II

Heart guiding head
Czech blood flooding America

Right to make left
Center to center at voting booth

Once you have it
You never lose it

Language as puzzle
Life as art

Maybe days will always be nights
In this bacon sky of twisted souls
And amended hearts

Honest tongue injures the broken few
But strengthens the rest
Like the Danube blue

Lead singer wannabe
Thespian with thousand faces

Losing laurels to politics and poetry
Like vanquished bullfighter to royal red

Chasing dreams like butterflies
Ideals like clouds
Minutes like motion

Sometimes time carries no wallet
Only seconds seared on forbidden master
Like sand on sacred soil

Rainbow

While today I cannot see
The ocean as it rises beyond the sea

The day will come when Jesus will be

And you and I will flee
The cages that we built for free

Like ribald rats that join the artillery

We are no more than rugged
Shadows feeling angry

Running amuck among the mortar and bricks
Like cousins without sticks
It is only when we click our heels
That the islands come to feel

Like languid soldiers left to steal

We know it requires grace
To love ourselves and the human race

But can we soften the edges enough
To grow a mind that thinks beneath the snow West of Winter

No lightning bolts on the horizon
Encores without a reason
Pennies short of a bargain
Love too slow to imagine
Rain to thick for the season

For in the embers of the fire
The decisions are made without ire
Our feet in the mire

Before Jesus
The wheel
Were oceans and eels
My time to heal

Like so many crevices and crannies
Our hearts alight with midnight
And devour the flower of this
Lonely and forbidden hour

On the street animals growl
Men cry foul
But in the end it matters little
For birds descend at dawn
Light canaries on an empty lawn

Razor

Beneath the armor of the moment
Lies the scar from the past
Lunging and licking its
Gargoyle head I find
Thumbs where fingers once were
And holes instead of eyes

This air
This now

Lingers and lounges
Like lost lepers in
Lunatic limousines or

The kind of Cannibal candescence
Carcasses condone and
College campuses connect to
Quiet quandaries
By collected carnations

This oxygen
This present
Given to mood swings of
Timbre and time
Rubber and rhyme

Rebel Rouser

7/16/15

In this moment
Love broken
Time taken
Fame mistaken
God bacon

I am king of the boulevard
Emperor of the street
Ruler of the avenue

Rules do not faze me
Laws but daze me

In this crucible of cacophony
I am the rooster and the roustabout

The rebel and the river
The very reason for hell's design
Purgatory's paucity

The unruly waves
Unwashed graves

And I make my way
Through the wicked waters and
Corroded caskets
As if tomorrow were today and

The cobwebs of my mind
Never mattered
Until, that is,
They mattered much more than mercy

Red Velvet

Words gliding like leather
Magenta to blue back to crimson

Reality roustabout
Fantasy feline
Dialogue dromedary

Sparrows chirping in the morn
Buffalo gathering at noon
Children misunderstanding June

Bard befitting the Greeks
Love, laughter and lore
Not of this orb

Karma exclaim
Desert rain
Oasis sane
Beefcake bane
Lacking shame

Language like lion
Racing beneath moon
On slightest of dunes

English playwright sucking soil of soul
Substance like silk
Power not poetry

Passing syntax and story
At old Globe lorry
William Shakespeare would have loved the blues
Without taking as much as a cue

Religion

Praying to the cross in church
Some despise you for it

Many do not understand
Others say they are spiritual
Believing in what exactly?

I believe that Jesus Christ
Died for our sins

I have for 40 years

At least I pray
Go to church
At least at least
I do not have a secret
When it comes to my religion

I am Catholic
 I am a sinner
I get new life
Through confession and communion

Not hate and violence

I believe in peaceful protesting
The non violent kind

I will pray for you
If you pray for me

I pray to Jesus on Sunday
And try not to forget him
The rest of the week

Mary and Joseph
In little Bethlehem

Jesus
The Son of God
Lying in manger

I believe it
I know it
I will not doubt it

Remnants of Love

This is beyond compromise
Beyond highs and lows

This is eyes drowning in salt water
Cups shaking till they spill drink

This is death disguised as life
Drums beating down a dark corridor

This is the 1980's poisoned
The Beatles murdered in 1968

I loved her till she left
Now I blame myself

After the gunpowder cleared
The skeleton of love awoken

The ocean is still wet
The desert dry

The sky is still blue
But my heart

Is like a jigsaw puzzle
Marched on by Nazi boots

Right versus Left

3/8/15

In this war of extremes
A balance is overlooked

The gray is a target
From blue and red

A diamond
Between two talking heads

The right likes the Bible
The left Jim Morrison's fable

The right is called conservative
The left liberal

Both believe in God
The one dollar bill

Neither can agree
As to what kind of God
Both are led by his spirit
One towards a right to life
The other a right to choose

One calls themselves Democrat
The other Republican

Right to left or left to right
We carry a heavy heft
To prove adept

Rhythm

Open mind
Living in time

Writing does not stop
Thinking endures

Hard life
On difficult planet

Something larger than yourself
Firing flame
Feeding future

Do not say no to anything
But violence and hate

Daddy I see your
Turquoise two

Mommy
I will write in oasis
The way you should have

The harvest on this purgatory
Proving pundits' paucity

Rhythm and Bile

We people subway cars and busses from here to there
Like little monsters looking for a school
Or termites dangling on the edge of a stool
Building wooden fools on high
Falling into scattered pools that die

Seek God they tell me
Find Jesus and you will be saved

But I keep praying
And nothing happens

Keep going to church
And life gets worse

Talk to therapists and priests
Then wonder if I don't already
Know more than them

Try to love myself
But find love as elusive as water

Don't beat myself up
But find big holes in the plastic nonetheless

What are the answers?
Where do I find them?

The Devil runs through my thoughts every 24
And I don't even know why
I try to keep him away

I do the best I can to muster an ounce of grace
On this planet my mother called purgatory
This dusty alabaster orb of blood and dime

All I wish for these days is a full glass of wisdom
And just a little peace on earth

Rigid Religion

2/24/15

Tomahawk the sun
Murder the moon

In between rants
Come ragged raves

Like lost man on an island
Silent brave

I feel the unencumbered day
Lay on this uncontested bray

Bible will not save the fray
Lying beneath the unmitigated gray

I ask you Christian counselor man
Why stay at this polluted bay
Water flows like wet hay
In your church of manipulated May

Ripping Rounds

By the cool lake I
Towel off the screams of yesterday
With the blanket of tomorrow

The island of wounded gorillas
Falls out of my nightmare and
Into my daydream
Like the difference between can and cannot

Vivid and stout
The self consciousness grows
Ever present
Ever true

Climbing trees without branches
Eels into mansions

I would rather the
Regret of absence
Than the pain of presence

The filet mignon of being
Than the sirloin steak of knowing

Rocking the Roll

11/23/14

Music leaving stage
Finding eardrums
Like smoke finds nose

They tell me the poetry is
Bleak and depressing

They cannot read more than one or two poems

They wonder about me
And what I don't see
I should just let it be

Locating love amid dusk's high
Darkness' rhubarb pie

Among the fingers and thumbs of Jesus' cry
Rocking to roll
Eating the scrim of our fantasy world
Laying bear the polluted streams
Of our ravaged rivers and oceans

I hear the drum beat
I sense the bass neat
Under the band's golden feet
Please Lord help me to be free in this bleacher seat

Rodgers and Hammerstein

Musicals like soaring eagles
Love a gleaming roller coaster
America shines without lantern

Lyrics like loaded lions
Music unmolested by mystical monsters
Muses marking mirrored memory
God galloping like golden gazelle
Sleeping on side of sun

One scotch tape
The other glue
A brand new hue

Meshing like moss
Multiplying like mass
Matriculating like Moses

Maybe theatre is not true
Or sky not blue

Time has spoken
Work stands test
Like very best
Unbroken

Run Don't Walk

In this gargoyle tongued abyss I sit

Waiting for bliss
While the world goes amiss

I stare at the peppermint oceans
The vanilla clouds

Like a clown called Javiar
I pounce on caviar

Always knowing
Forever sowing

In-between the teeth of time
January sublime
The raven winged troubles of the day
Disappear like madmen without a say

Never sullied
Never screamed

I awake with the monster at my back
Reeling from a shark attack

Saving My Life

Poetry has saved my life
Like water on a searing day
In the desert
Rice to bloated bellies in Africa

I can write it whenever I want
Wherever I want
In a coffee shop
Silent room or
Crowded discotheque

Writing takes me away from reality
Me away from me
Lets me create and feel
Whatever I want

It allows me to breathe life
Into my words and
Wondering whereabouts
Like a mechanic recharges an old Buick
And the heart surgeon gives life to
A doubtful patient

Poetry makes me happy
To have finished what I started
And touched others with it

I know my life
Has made a difference

And I can die peacefully

Sergeant Slaughter

7/4/15

He walks the beat
With leaden feet

Like a marine on the street
Who does not greet

A wicked bird
Without a word

This tug of war
Bends my very soul

As the one I love
Cries to be whole

In this island in the sun
Without coal

Ripping to rip
Is an awkward slip
For this army of one
That is not quite done

As for you and me
There is three

If you count the sun
And how it shines

But does not run
On this mountain of none

Shedding Shackles

In the potent rivers of the mind
The sketch comedy skit of rhyme
Runs away with time

Like a redwood of name
This doctor of fame
Lives for the game

Red sunsets
Aqua skies
The dream has eyes

Beelzebub lies
His belt has thighs
Handcuffs rise
Beneath the prize

Jesus by night
Asinus by day

Cage birds
Capture herds

Detail moves
Chaos grooves

Running and rolling
Into a grave
Filled with the brave

She Left Me Tonight

Tonight the dagger sticks
The bridge is in sight

The tongue licks
The wounds it has made

I cannot write anymore
The night is cold with regret

I do not want loneliness
Its cold branches and ragged roots

I wish for love
Its open palms and tender refrains

I do not care if you hurt me ten times ten
I will come back ten times eleven

Others may say what they do
But I care only for you

Rugged words
Belying gentle deeds

Please come back
I wish to caress your face

Gaze into turquoise eyes
Run fingers through brunette hair

Without you dead I would be
Like the train tracks I
Embrace upon learning of your demise

Short Poem

A little ditty for my child of the city
In those black pants
Ever so pretty

Down by the river
The skin of you glows
Like moon dust

Under the tree
You lie in the meadow

The sun colors and carves
Your oblong face
Like a Van Gogh masterpiece

Cotton candy lips
Kissing brandy sips
Above swivel hips
Surfing Pistachios rips

Your wave never dips
Or slips
Dearest Patricia

Sidewalk of Song

Talent agents all in a row
Talking about things they don't know
Giving birth to a new low

Sign me because
I am not talented enough
Don't sign me
Because I am too talented

Tell me what you know
When you have not played the game
When the battlefield
Is for others to learn

When fighting for a cause
Takes a backseat to making money
Smile turned upside down
Cavities conning cranium

Please Mr. talent agent
Do not slumber
The nights are short
The compromises large
The space between the two
As thin as the smoke that masks your fall

Sister Once More

Hands softer than wheat
Harder than the stare you
Bounce off the bedroom wall

Hair golden as sunbeam
Beautiful girl

Smile bending at corners
Like abandoned lover

If you ever need me
I am there

If you do not forsake me
The penguin wears no clothes

Do not shun me
For I am barely whole

My agitation
My gutted soul

My anger
I lose control

Open your ears to me
Your eyes

I am attached to the world
Your cries

Perhaps there is still a chance for us
My mother of a dance

A tomorrow for this today
A rocket in space
For every losing face

A shooting star
That precedes our fall from grace
1, 825 days
A tenth of my life

60 months of strife

I have lost you

My battered heart
Withers like a rose

Runs like year old pantyhose

I do not ask much
But this I do

Give me a chance to repaint the past
Open a dialogue like
Reagan and Gorbachev

Like we had as children at our
Little house on Calhoun Street
In uptown New Orleans

Like we should
Like we deserve

Because not to try
Would be akin to death squared
Love unbared
Genius not dared

Sabrina my little sister
Open those turquoise two
And let me in

Lay down the sword
And take up the hoe

Shred the armor
Swallow the lord

Now not then
Passion and Zen
Like a red hen

Fill the void
With my pen

Sister, Sister

In the hall of poems
Some add
Some subtract

And some carry your spirit
Like coal miners looking
For victims in a collapsed mine

You have not been there for me
For almost forever
This I know to be true

Why I cannot say
I almost wish I did not know
As you pull away
Like Santa on his sleigh

I love you
But no longer think
You love me

And that cuts deeper than
Razor to wrist

You who tackled
Boys three times your size
In improvised football games
Near old Tulane Stadium
In Uptown New Orleans
Where we lived

The wall in your bedroom filled with
Blue first place ribbons
From school track and field meets

Then high school
And we managed to
Keep the chord
Untangled and untarnished

But college came
And me in my punk rock garb
And you in your sorority sweater
Did not mesh

You did not invite me to your wedding
And the avalanche began

It will end in the ocean
Made of our tears

Once we realize that life
Is too short
To sashay in the shadows

Sister Sister Sister

In the pit of lyme
That tastes like time

I ride a caboose
To the other side of rhyme

This piece of art
That is life
Dances like a mime and
Costs a dime

We are the polluted
In rivers and valleys we skip
That we will not sip

Sister dearest
Where are you?

Your cherry lips
Sitting by a dip
In your latest slip

Like a lost maiden
Without a flip

Tanning those golden California hips
I will never grip

Sky

I walk you when you are wet
I gallop through your rough edges
When I am frightened

I slide down your smooth stomach
When I am happy

Casanova caught
Hamlet harassed

You are lightning yellow
Tomato red
Sidewalk gray

Your ocean of blue
Waterfall of orange

Blaze through uneven hues

When I look up
Romeo is ravaged
Jesus jammed

Big, bountiful and beatific
The Rolling Stones could not
Touch you with Mick Jagger's presence
Or Keith Richards' fingers

The Maker is caught up in you
Like some sort of butterfly to blue

Like my grandparents did the Czech flag too
And I the red, white and blue of you
Pauper turning prince

I touch you every moment by not touching you
I make love to you every night
In corners of dark orange and black
Like the English do the Union Jack

Sky High

Red Robin sinking like celebrity centipede
Fast and forlorn

Falling stars lighting the
Horizon like peppermint ice cream

I tire of this town
And its goldfish bowl traffic
Mountain low mediocrity

Neighborhoods on the edge of nihilism
Politicians pocketing popularity
Not perfection

Hollywood hot then cold
Thirty years of climbing
Only to descend like dog dripping

City of angels
You have lost your wings
And cherubic face

Once the goal
Now the mole

Once Oscar's role
Now a red carpet soul
Sputtering along like
God's least sacred knoll

Sleep

Wrists under hips
Shoulders next to lips

Night pouring light
Sight feeling fright

You putting up fight
Because I just might

Barreling stomach into ribs
Like octopus

The TV cannot exist without an assist

Pillow commercial
Evangelist valley
Transmission test
Down the alley

Your eyes gazing into mine
Like waterfalls cascading

Your thighs
But lies
I will not rise
Winning door prize
Slowing ember dies

Another night
Absent of highs
Coming on the edge of sighs

Song of Life

8/23/15

Rambling through golden meadow
Like storm without yield
Emperor not kneeled
Football player unhealed

Gall not making for wall
Like governor's call or
President's fall

Mental illness never deflating ball
Talent tall

Nine years in Los Angeles
To next haul

Trauma turning to truth
Turbulent tummy wisdom tooth

No children
Ex-wife
Fiancé in new life

Steep climb
Through desert and slime
Not enough to obliterate rhyme

For in the end
Water and dime
Cushion time
Like Adam's mime

Standing in Line at the DMV

Maybe I should not drive
Just use fairy dust or
Twitch my nose like
Elizabeth Montgomery in Bewitched

Slammin' shoe soles
On vanilla bean concrete
Like Blue Whale alabaster nose

Drivers moving slowly
Like arthritic crow
Or story by Edgar Allen Poe

Falcon soaring
My head belongs somewhere else

But if I have learned anything
It is that even this is poetry

Starbucks

Oasis in middle of North Hollywood desert

Writing here almost every day
Career in balance

Would rather write among others than by myself

Friends I meet
Beautiful women I talk to
Priscilla, the new manager, takes charge

Raul, Mimi, Liz, Kelly, Daniel and Sarah friends who work here

Corporation that treats people like human beings
Everyone knows who you are

Inspiration for bleeding words
Onto empty page

Starbucks on Camarillo and Tujunga
In North Hollywood
Turns dreams into dazzle
Heart into overdrive

Like a space shuttle taking off
Lover finding balance between

Loving himself and
Giving to one he loves

Little coffee shop
You have altered my existence

Like the difference
Between asphalt and vanilla
Vacuum and viscus

Street Master

Shakespeare of suburbia
Breaking rule
Not law

Climbing broken promise
Like priest certain silence

Convicted killer
Suffocated stardust

Walking skid row's atomic bomb blast
Like lunar landing
Complete and conjoined

Sailor with a broken mast
Astronaut without a past

Street master
Dropping nickel on look
Dime on book

No boss
No pension
No portfolio extension

Sleeping in mud
Like uneven spud

Dingo dust
Inglorious must

Rust kills faster
Than dirt ever will

Perhaps popularity
Poisons peacock

Tired tan
Like timid tundra

Behind ego is

Everyman
Waiting for window and water
Jazz is Jesus
Cross nailing flesh
Ruby lips half of mesh

Beating rock on
Polyester picnic table

Street wrapped in satin and silver
Like crystal water pouring
Into golden geyser

Forest and feather
Sleeping on black leather

Street master
Ballroom blaster

Seeking sapphire melody
Finding sacred mediocrity

Strip Solid

At the Coffee Bean on
Sunset and Heyworth near Fairfax and
The Sunset Strip

Europeans converge like
Muffins and cupcakes

Liberals all
They detest the local mall
And Texas tall

While celebrating America's experiment
In the hostel hall

They dine on Doritos and Big Macs
Not comprehending their own fall

Half Czech
Half Austrian
Mostly American

I understand
Like guru on call
Romantic and pragmatic static

Dvorak versus agnostic
Gershwin meeting Napoleon
The ghetto brawl
The Parisian gall

Mother and father dying
With Czech flag in teeth
Never realizing they were complete

The only boy in my family
Flogged like scapegoat in the pall

I will not weather
I will not stall

They can blackball me
I will not be deterred

They can cuff me
My ideals will not be shackled

They can commit me
My voice will not be silenced

I will run this marathon like a sprinter
Taking this blessed path
Like a screaming monk
Doing the math

Subtotal

34 years of performing on stage
Page

This moment is creative
The middle is the beginning

My voice is clear
Uncluttered
Not desperate
Poised
Ready to be unsteady

Obstacles hurdled
Time stopped
Nights not lost

I need someone to take a chance on me
On real talent
On the kind of courage that
Can change the world

The type of love that comes around
Once every century

Someone without blinders
Who puts people before money
Ability before liquidity

Who I can call a friend
While I am on the mend

Sue the Sky

7/10/15

I am the sky
It is me

Living in fits of feeling
Tears of tragedy

I am the sea
It is me

Existing in handfuls of emotion
Avenues of exaggeration

I am the land
It is me

Putting down roots
Like a tattered sail
Still moving
In drops of delight

The psychiatrists and doctors
Cannot measure
The hugs in my heart or
The dogma of my days

Let them practice
For they must

But never forget
The sound of the spirit
The saga of the sage
The guile of the guide
The guilt of the guru or
The fingertips of the sun

Summer Afternoon

The tree in front of my third floor apartment in North Hollywood
Blooms like a pregnant mother
The yellow and green leaves nearly touching the living room window

The poetry on my tongue
Scaling tallest peak
Turning other cheek
Gathering life oblique

Writing for steady glands and unsure hands
The swan and not the story

Words flowing through my veins like blood
Circling lions in African sun

Images dropping from my imagination like rain
Speeding like a wet train
Empty paper filled with clues
Like a busy muse

The sun orange yellow
The sky red
The moon full
The asphalt on the 405 bending in the heat like my temper

This day before dusk carrying me
Towards the cradle of cancer where the
Alcohol, drugs and cigarettes
That sometimes fuel a poem
Are replaced by love

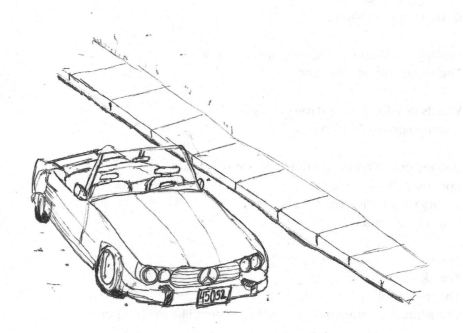

Sun Beam Lost Dream

As the sun sets
The world begets

2 am as dark as African skin
As lonely as Times Square
On January 1st

This summer of peace
This lover of the lonely hour

Embracing skulls and souls
Like lulls and holes

I once loved a girl
Who did not wish to be loved

She swirled and sashayed
Through the Jamoca Almond Fudge of life

Like a street urchin
Without a map

A teddy bear
Taking a lap

Maybe she had no love sheet of rap

Born in the back of
Some metaphysical gap

Loving her
Till my last nap

This season of love
Three months from above

Descending lightly like a dove
I now love another
Like Romeo his Juliette
Trolilus his Crescida

This 93 days of tans and tanks
Beaches and bombs
Not wrinkling my heart

Wars always will be
We will never not be free
To change what we see

Like dolphins
Swimming quickly in the sea

Battling the mirror
Two halves of me

One dark
The other light

Which one do I keep in sight
On this summer night?

This summer does not end
Flowing into space
Without a trace

Flying and feeling
Surfing and grieving
Frolicking and fleeting

It is H2o
Salt water swimming
Street hockey

Yearning for tranquility
Between nations, races and religions

The kind that comes
With harmony of the soul and mind

No more bloodshed
Politicians misled
Dark days ahead

System singing
Like Olympic rings
Beautiful things

Believing in the
Mighty sting
Either wing

Under the orange red sun
I love you
Like no other

Like the yogurt moon above
Building bridges
Detonating walls

Galloping through empty spaces
With your face in the gallows

Your presence in my being
Your skin on mine
Our fingers intertwining
Loving you once
To love you ever more

Needing you forever
Wanting you always

Holding you this summer of peace
Syria, Ukraine, Israel and Iran
Do not matter .

Your ocean blue eyes
Like silver fireflies
Shapely arms like feathered branches
Golden legs like supple ranches

Sipping some Hillary to find reality

Bending over a bush and
Some green Donald

Psychiatrist telling me that
I am at a breaking point

Fracturing all angles
This summer of peace
With angels and architects
Working like assets
Firing up the Barbecue
Unfurling the American flag

Never perfect
Sagging not
Like some thousand pound rag
Sitting in the park
On the Fourth of July

Firecrackers exploding
Like reality shows

Lighting up the sky
Like dictators with nothing but foes

Summer of peace
Soldier of our best

Letting me down not
Leading me down not
Unraveling path

Naked in thy sunlight

Your very cloudburst
Longer days
Ancient bays
No delays

You are a chain reaction
Summer of peace
Putting arms down
Others following

Loving you flaws and all
You loving me
Laws on call

Talking about peace
Words mattering not

A culture of peace to grease

An understanding leasing
A language unfleecing

Summer of love
Swimming to me
Like a fallen groom

Coming to me
Like a darkened room

Surrounding me like light
Next to me like night
Holding onto me like a tattered kite

Summer right
Like August bite
Into dawn like an early flight
Double vision like salient sight
Early July like swelled might
Twilight like June height

I am white and tight
Love to write

During this summer of peace
Uncanny trip to Nice

Grabbing swimsuit
Stepping over jellyfish

Hurried and hard
Running down the shore

Another Isis attack in the news
Giving me the blues

At my back
One more shark attack

Lessening the bloodshed
Harkening the love fed

Furthering the peaceful words said
Not the soil spread

Finding gray between
Black and white

Not a missile in my back yard
No one understands
Not even the bard

This summer of peace
Under a canopy of release
Ringing truer than
A gambler's favorite card

Rock hard
Without any lard

Remembered as the one with teeth
The emperor's wreath

The sun in the distance
The moon full as a gun

If not the world as one

Sunday Before the TV Screen

After turning on
What I should be turning off

First downs dance in my head
Like redundant lovers

Pointing the way to tornados of tumult
Earthquakes of earnestness
Truth lingers in silence on the field

Helmets cracking
Shoulder pads smacking

A high school basketball coach once told me
That you have to be crazy to play football

This chess match that got me through
The bullies and name calling of eighth grade

That connected me with
What life erased and divided

That which I will never get back
This grid iron of wills and skills
That takes my mind
From the wars and strife
Marking this cotton candy blue orb

Until I have the courage to turn it off
And sit still as
Cardboard on sofa

Unable to weep for the sins
Quarterbacks commit while throwing
Interceptions behind enemy lines

Sundays with Stephen

12/4/14

He has a German name
A gift from God
An acoustic guitar with strings as sturdy as Abraham

He wears two pairs of scuffed shoes
And the same worn pair of jeans every week

He tells me that therapy speaks to him
And it probably does

But I know that if he devoted the same time
He does to music as he does to his practice
He would be on the Billboard charts

Stephen sweats when he sings and plays
But never perspires when he talks

Stephen, oh, Stephen is a God among men
The problem is he would rather not admit it to himself
The truth can be a difficult thing to look at

But when he does his genius will blossom into more than
Two chairs in a room

Supreme

1/13/15

I do not want to die
Want to live forever

I do not have to be rich
Do not have to be famous

I want to make a difference
Touch as many lives as possible

Climb through every loophole
Clear every hurdle

The orange in the sky
Mirrors the orange in your eyes
Like tiny bullets of rust

Dusk falls on open mouths
Raised to the clouds
Like angry fists

Justice cannot wait
I climb it like a mountain
Scale it like a ladder

Fall like a leaf

Telling my Mother and Me
that the Holocaust Did Not Happen
on a Flight from Austria

3/7/15

The man sitting between my mother
And me on a flight from Vienna to
London told her that the
Holocaust did not happen.

"Nein," he said. "Es war nicht."

My mother, who lived in Czechoslovakia during WWII,
And saw Adolf Hitler close the doors of
The National Dramatic Conservatory
Where she studied and acted the Greeks and
Shakespeare in 1943

Who had Jewish neighbors who
Were there one day and gone for good
The next

Told him that the Holocaust was real.

"Es war echt," she said in remarkably good German.

The man was startled for a moment
But continued to deny the existence
Of any concentration camps during the war.

My mother stood up in mid-air
And walked to the rear of the plane.

It was her way of speaking her
Truth, however she could, wherever she could.

Later she sat down in the aisle seat again
And looked at me.

Her face a mosaic of sorrow and sweat
Confidence and clarity

Her eyes beaming love
Her hands life

Ten Minutes Before

Ten minutes before
The Starbucks
On Camarillo and Tujunga
In North Hollywood closes

Ten minutes before
Peace and tranquility
Turn to trembling fingers
And open blisters

Ten minutes before
Iced coffee and Passion tea
Turn to Budget Gourmets
And Totino's pizza rolls

Ten minutes before the laughter dies
And the screaming begins

Ten minutes before
Gays and straights
Sitting together
Turns into gays and straights
Sitting apart

Ten minutes before
Love walks out the glass door
And kindness is confronted
By the tomahawk of hate

Ten minutes before ten minutes barely
Matters anymore

Tentacles

12/8/14

I hear them
Before they hear me

Before the wind
In the shadow
Careens around my throat

Like the black chocolate
In the armor under my hand

Wide and thick
Narrow and thin
Like sin

They mark the streets
Like crows pecking

Seagulls digging into dumpsters

Wrapping thumbs and spine
Around my neck

Fingers and forks
Fixed at the dinner table

Maybe daddy won't scream
At mommy tonight

And make me manipulate
Maximum cover from forlorn faces
Furious and frowning on the banks of their tears

Terror Tower

8/18/15

On the 102nd Floor of
One World Observatory
People hardly matter

Cities disintegrate
States converge
Countries disappear like
Spare change from a hole in
My jean pocket

Ghosts and glances
Climbing walls
Tickling clouds
Punching sky
Paradise pinching Peoria

Intercepting instinct
Exploding like hand grenade

Oh, Freedom Tower of swan and Sandy
Song and Gandhi
Steam and Mandy

Eyes hear
Ears see
Days fade
Hours made
Atoms invade

That Poem

Breaking away is as hard as soap
Often without hope
Transcending even the pope

Dialing dormant digits
I am the wolf at the door
The very doorman on the floor

And then there is that poem
Waking patience
While forsaking the green, green
Grass of your face

The stirring of scars
The leaping of lemons
The rolling of ribbons

And that poem
As hard as that hill to master
As ridiculous as rhyme to rule

Ripping chords in forest of swords
Like an antidote to lords
Who pounce blue Fords
Into backyards of hordes
Behind maybe a yesterday of
Sinking towards

For this is but poetry on an island of fanatical feline frazzled
Fiords bending backwards
To belch bricks like billy clubs

The Beast of Least

I hate
When I skate
Down the wrong grate

When what falls
Torridly calls

When my blessings
I do not await

The flooded lungs amount

Like warriors
On a fount

Day by day
I learn to pray

I am the choir boy
By the bay

When I decide to stay
On the avenue
Where the clay
Is black and white and
Not gray

The Dance

The tango of now
Kisses the brow of wow

As declarations come and go
Faith wanes
Like a high jacked beau

With you I waltz
On the dance floor of
An abstract foe

We foxtrot
Like electric antelopes
On bruised islands of
Forestry and fog

There was a time
We sped down corridors of grog
Like spiders on a log

But now we groove at
Discotheques of sound
Like bards of a noun

Sometimes the truth finds us
Rolling and rocking
Beneath the ground
Like alligators
In some 4 am pound

The End

The scars that touch my soul
Like naked men do come and go

Not knowing once
Not knowing twice

Why are fingers knit so slow
Or our passions do not flow

The wall I climb today
Maybe the same I leave at bay
Jumping jumping into the fray
My face on burning dock place

Rumbling rumbling within space
Only to see my life disgraced
By leaping elves and tired dwarfs
Who in the end do not walk my halls

In this clock of every day
I sense the ribald cock screaming hay

Over there where hours stop
She tells me that she cannot pay
For the pain she brought my way

In the back alleys I drop the gray
For just once I find the clay
Just enough to seize the day
On this orb where I dare not stay

The Girl in the Spool

At the Coffee Bean
On Chandler and Lankershim
In North Hollywood
The girl next to me
Plays with midnight hair
Underneath hood

One leg working better
Than other

She keeps green luggage
Under table
As if she has somewhere to go
But all day to get there

She pulls out a small mirror and
Puts on mascara

I have a feeling
That she is a stray and
I have a bad history with strays

Pink fingernails
White designer bag
She hovers over
Empty small coffee

Orange covered diary
The lithe creature
Keeps stuffing items
In and out of her bag

She asks to use my cell phone
After telling her
To keep it short I let her use it

She says she has been waiting on a friend
For two hours

Am I too nice?
Is niceness a sign of weakness?

Or am I too busy being a North Star
For everyone to see?

She leaves two hours later
Hardly uttering a word

I stay until the coffee shop closes

The Jet Blue Experience

8/4/15

Here in seat 28D on the aisle
Of Jet Blue flight 124
From Los Angeles to New York City
The bathroom doors open and close
Like lifelong foes

The shaking never ends
For this corporeal punishment
In the air does not mend

Give me Delta
American
United

One last stand
In a metal tube
That does not bend

An airline that does not lend
A name
To this noble end

Then disappoint
Like some turbulent bent

Passengers hitting my arm
At least 30 times
On the way to the lavatory
Not one says I am sorry

More of them went twice
Than I have ever seen
It seems they were more nervous
Than me

Traveling 3000 miles
For a fee
Made more expensive because
It seemed like free

The Last Poem

2/28/15

There has to be a last poem
One that sums up
All that went before

Rips and dips
Moves and grooves

A lasting memory of
The burning sun poetry is

The aching hearts it relieves
The adolescents it rescues
The teachers it inspires
The poets it saves

There has to be a last poem

One that sums up
The troubles on a planet
Made of atoms and molecules
Populated by Gods and sinners

The Very Last Poem

This poem
The very last in this book
Bites and soothes
Writes and moves

Others cannot live my life for me

I must decide
My thoughts and actions
Deeds and misdeeds

I must choose
What to do with my talents
How best to serve myself and others

This poem
The very last of this book
Meanders and curves
Slides and swerves
But never crashes

The beauty in me
Outshines the ugly

The good the bad
The messy the sad

Therapy

All in or all out
Not half a pout

Embracing the third realm
Under the broken elm

Like crossword puzzle
In the dark

I admire your bark
Listening to the wise lark

Freud or Jung
Both unsung

Many do not believe
Nor do they fear to grieve

Mirror does not lie
Takes you out of Bed Stuy

To change world
I must change myself first

That is more difficult
Than an adrenaline burst

These Halls

11/24/14

These halls are vanilla covered

Doctors, orderlies and nurses
In white sashaying to appointed rounds

Medication slipped under tongue
Like junior mint

This crazy cathedral
Nut house
Mental hospital

Open for business

Mental illness muscling
Metaphor and Metamucil
Like Egg Mcmuffin order #363

Mental patients
Housed and fed like cattle
But are they ill in a world that drives just about everyone a little over the edge?

No, daddy, I won't admit myself to make you and my sister happy

These halls as neutral as lab coats

They

In the bushes and brothels
They hide
Tending to their side

In the alleys and avenues
They get by
Smiling an aside

On the beaches and broad streets
They find the answer
To their slide

They sleep on trains
In the monsoon rain
Like bane from another stain

Children fear them
Authorities jeer them
Rebels cheer them
For a while

Lunatics and lizards
Sleeping in loony bins and lounges

Eating left over Lasagna for lunch

We should not glow
A world weary know
Like worms after a drenching

The middle child
During a benching

Silent slaves moving quicker than light
Faster than a midnight wrenching

Walking like criminals
Breathing like decimals
Angry like animals

Licking tears like red wine
Blood like wooden cross divine
Please crawl up my supple spine
Only love buys them time
In this holy land sublime

This Book

Does not have one bad poem in it

Makes my daydreams
Bite at night

Is what I have always
Wanted from a tome of mine

Displays some basic truths
Like dignity squared
And talent bared

Does not pretend to
Be about poetry
It is poetry

Is an act of love
A work of art

Mends broken souls
Fills barbaric holes

This Girl

Puts me between hell and purgatory
But never heaven

She wants to be served
Worked for

But she serves
Works for no one

She is another woman
Sent to make me suffer for my sins

I sometimes hate her
Often resent her
And more and more feel vanilla towards her

She is not Mother Mary
Or nurse Nightingale
But an actress who rarely acts

A lover of celebrity
Who uses it not to be one

A red carpet Juliet
Who never gets on one

Because E.T. is more important than IQ

This Thing Called Poetry

I have to believe
Like a cop going undercover
That something good will come

That no matter how many hurdles
I put in the way
Diamonds are about to appear

Gold is about to be found
Rhyme is on the way
Simple words save the day

Alliteration and assonance
At play
I have to want it
Like a dog a bone
Or his favorite sofa throne

And I have to believe that I
Am worthy to receive it

Because all of us have a
Beautiful side
If we believe that we do

If the good in us
Outweighs the bad
And the happy the sad

This Time

9/6/15

Birds chirp
Monkeys clap
Aliens rap

Avenues and boulevards are clean
Like a nativity scene

Shaking palms
Trembling knees
Coiled stomach
Disappear into the sea
Like lost house keys

Heads turn
Eyes burn
Legs churn

This time
Voices are loud
Stares long
Opinions unbowed
Crowds wowed

Herds die
As gurus lie
Scholars vie for the sky
Philosophers get high on why

I march to a different drummer
Like that musician Joe Strummer

Through It All

Through every thorn and
Broken bone

I give you refuge
Like an injured refugee on a sinking dingy
A soldier losing his leg to a mine

I have doubted you
You have wondered about me

I would rescue you from
A raging fire
A homicidal maniac
Perhaps even yourself

Through it all
Every syllable Shakespeare wrote
Idea Aristotle had
Rage between you and me
Emotions murdered

We made it through

The rain retired
For another day

Somehow tears of joy
Even veiled
Are stronger than trembling palms

Time for Myself

Minutes for me
Seconds sacking Seroquel
Days dodging distant dingos

Time to uncomplicate
The complicated

Sew a tapestry
Of nimble meditation

Knit a blanket
Of unmitigated contemplation

Then rip it apart
With scissors and pick
Only to improvise the kick

Full moon to walk under
Sun bursting through window
Like naked narcissist

Time with me not free
A path not of economy

Toes and Woes

On the tip of the foot
The ego suffers no fools

No uncommon common visitors
From beneath

No relentless passengers wrapped
Around its heel

We buy bread to eat jam
Purchase butter to consume bagels

The coffee shops of yesterday are like feet

They have sprouted many toes

Asked too many questions
Of the wrong people
At the wrong time

And died for their abandon

Do we follow suit?
Do we give at the office?

On the top of the foot
We realize that skin makes us
Our own worst enemy

Together

I spent a day with my love
My love alone

My feather in lightest air
Her countenance ever so fair

We talked of love
We spoke of now
We chatted about
Things we usually
Do not have time
To talk about

Our stomachs full
Faces needing little pull
She and I ventured
Into deepest cool
Like two kittens
Playing with wool

Hours studying her eyes
Helped me realize
They are fuller than fireflies

Towards Something

They tell me I am running away again
I say I am moving towards something

It is time to go back to
New York City
Tumult and tranquility
Harassment and humility

Leave Los Angeles
Door by the store
Killer of cake
Baker I forsake

Rough seas
Bad knees
Solemn fees

Skid row
Slauson and San Pedro
Murder mime
Plant time

Frantic fears faced
Hills maced

I need the Northeast, the corridor
D.C., Philly, Boston
This eight year diversion
I do not sing its song
I am too strong

Trembling fingers subside
Laughter abides

New York
I slowly sashay to your summers

Leaving my elbows in L.A.

Transition Period

Between hedge and hog
Lies the river of return
Where princes and paupers go to die

And the only reason jazz is not Judas
Is that the trombones have more treble
And less tenacity

The innocent laugh over there like cackling geese
While the guilty binge
On Brie and Camembert

Somewhere God is weeping
Under collapsing bridges
And cracking freeways

I moved to Los Angeles to act
Nothing so far

I ran to tinsel town for validation
So far none

I did standup comedy in Hollywood
For red carpets and dollar bills
But got neither quickly

Maybe this is a transition period between then and now
Present and past
Europe and America
But only if I am aware of it as I go along

As it rolls into another December
And yet another year

I am who my father warned me about

Transparent Tiger
(Dedicated to Nicki Minaj)

Cotton candy lips
Bubble gum hips
Peppermint tongue

Transparent tiger
Reason for the reason
Pattern behind the tapestry

Form addictive
Figure reactive
Fists never restrictive

Mind marries mist
Dove dancing list
Words with you make me wonder
Winding like stranded warriors

Protection low
Eyes glow

Hands new
Swords free

2 a.m. hair
I will not stare
Only do my best to care

Trapped

9/7/15

Between cliffs and skiffs
Moats and boats
Like Jesus before dawn
Judas at dusk

Dreams and schemes
Your butterscotch cheeks
Wish they could redeem
Like lost weeks
Evenly steamed

Weight of air
Hint of stare
Like grizzly bear
Asleep in lair

Protected by rhyme
Hardly worth a dime
In this valley of grime

I look above
To his alabaster dove
It sends me no love

Soul a deep hole
Does not console

Evil and good
Made of wood
Midnight hood

Radomir Vojtech Luza

True

I brush my teeth with truth
The kind of saber only children know
And schizophrenics feel

Laboring under the freeway overpass
Like Johnny Carson after Joan Rivers or
Lenny Bruce after the arrest

Truth that sheds light on the
Pilfered past like Judas Iscariot
The double tongued then

Sincerity that bleeds buoyancy
And blame like the back of
My father's hand
Steeped in flesh and familiarity
That only she, my mother, comprehends

Honesty which texts when it
Cannot call and
Takes messages instead of
Nothing at all

Love that is the question as well
As the answer

Tulane

Momentum skydiving into fresh air
I was alive
Part of something larger than myself

Panting and prancing
To school each morning
Friends catching my fall

New Wave
Punk
Underground

Music rekindling a sense of belonging
Like family

Dancing until 3 am
Writing for newspapers
Disc jockeying for school station

Open my eyes Lord
To the possibility of this planet

The very Thoreau and Walden in backyard
Professors powering past
Porcupine pricking

After four years and a BA
Real world jabbing

I am artist
Reality upside down to downside up
Jobs returned in kind

Jackhammering patterns and prognosis
Like rusted rain

Mamma
I rarely saw you weep

Two

You and me in my car
Going where the breeze takes us
Where the beginning makes us

I cannot be without you
I cannot cannot learn to love you
Like John loved Yoko
And Jesus probably did Mary Magdalene

The truth flows in beautiful blue rivers
And flies through timid tundra skies
Like bulldog sniffing sidewalk
Or baboon beating breast

We sit at the Flame Broiler in
Downtown Los Angeles across from each other

Like trapped lovers in a cage

All I do these days is pray for me
Pray for you
And hope that like you did
Last night in my orange shirt of a nightgown you break into
Song at three in the morning

The two of us crying until we laugh

Near bathroom sink water flowing

Use Me

For my dreams
Seams and moon beams

Days swaying
Hours laying
Dramas paying
Boulevards fraying

Doctors imbibing gold
Artists in cold
Politicians corrupting like mold

Lunging and leaping
Like lunatics
For an ounce of my bold hold

Use me for
Your green tomorrow
Orange sun today

Nooks and crannies of time
Puncturing rhyme
Poisoning like slime

On this rotating orb
Of aqua and onyx
Purpose and grime
Lemon and lime

Use me because
I would rather be used
Than to use

Veil of Stale

Smells like old meat
Sounds like merry feet

Never not unhappy
On the island of Crete

I need a steady beat
Oh pastor give me Jesus' phone number
So we can meet

The present is defeat
The past I do not wish to greet

Someone somewhere take my hand
Lead me from these blood splattered thoughts

To the Garden of Eden where the devil is king
Of his own sting

But on this day
A step away
From what may
Be kept at bay

When I lay my body down to stay
On this field of gray
And golden hay

What once was stale
Dies in a ricochet of hail

Victory Song

7/30/15

Replace the seams with dreams
In this the city of our time

Los Angeles
You loaded beast
Looking for feast

The years have treated you
Like rising yeast

The homeless in your closet
Bring no defeat

They descend the stairs
Like torpedoed angels

The elongated streets and
Sheltered feet

Send you into a tailspin of
Balance and burrito

Second City
You love like no other
Four wheeled chariots
On white cement of free

Maybe just maybe
Hollywood too will see

Villains Valley

Bludgeoning beneath open coffins and
Closed quadrants

The brackets bargain
Like closed avenues
In the detours of the heart

Banging and begging
For stolen memories
On the stagecoach of rhyme sublime

The panther's jaw and lion's tail
Compete like a book of Braille

One finding sanity
The other a pail

Coiled muscles and foiled hustles

Not working with slime
Stopping in Brussels
Served on a dime with lime

Committing no crime
Before bending bushes
Made by time
Borrowed by a mime and
Murdered by rhyme

Waiting

3/16/15

In the bushes and backyards
The barrels and bundles
Of this love

I always come back to you
Lips soft as sofa
Hair curly as caterpillar

Time passes
As it always does
We notice
To hardly notice at all

The geometry and algebra
Of the past
We cared about yesterday

Today is difficult
Leading with right foot
Finishing with left

Oh Jesus
I love you
Forever waiting

Radomir Vojtech Luza

Waiting

While I wait
Open the gate
To fate

If not now
Then when

If not the castle
Why try?

Many do not understand
Some lend a hand

Tomorrow matters not
Yesterday an iron pot
Today all I got

All I have not said
Comes out in dimes and dollars
Rhymes and fodder

This voice cannot wait
For its mate

So I fight to the end
Without a bend

Knowing what I know
Doing what I do

Forever new
Never blue
I am one of a few

Wanting It

The drama builds
Like on those skid row LA streets

If you want fame and money
Passion outweighs depression
Desire does chance

Smoke gives way to fire
Trembling hands to no one's liar

If people are alike
Anyone can be a celebrity
Everyone can be on a magazine cover
The bold and unbowed survive

You have to want it
Blue eyes on prize

Frolicking fingers on finish line
Beige legs clearing hurdle upon hurdle

Breasts heaving
Stomach churning
Feet quivering
Heart yearning
Price burning

Wedding Bell Blues

Her legs shake
My hands tremble
We are giraffes with short necks

I am as confident
As an orange zebra in a yellow fashion show
As sure of myself as
A guitar in a symphony orchestra

She is more nervous these days
Than a rhyme in a sentence of ricochets

But through it all she is on my side
A gullible, gliding, gutsy lover
Who never says I love you first
But means it more second

The prima donna is not helping, it seems
But it hardly matters
Because mind over matter is

The moss is lifting
Cross falling
Fangs not proceeding

And we sit in a dark corner praying,
That what we do not know will not pollute what we do

West of Winter

No lightning bolts on the horizon
Encores without a reason
Pennies short of a bargain
Love too slow to imagine
Rain to thick for the season

For in the embers of the fire
The decisions are made without ire
Our feet in the mire

Before Jesus
The wheel
Were oceans and eels
My time to heal

Like so many crevices and crannies
Our hearts alight with midnight
And devour the flower of this
Lonely and forbidden hour

On the street animals growl
Men cry foul
But in the end it matters little
For birds descend at dawn
Light canaries on an empty lawn

Where Are You?

7/28/15

In the beckoning breach
That is this heart
I look asunder

You pick at the sky with children
In your teeth

I search beneath broken bramble
To find fingers lost in hands
Arms forgiven by torsos

In the spaces you do not see
The insane congregate
Criminals castrate
Animals disintegrate
Like Manatee at the shore

Yearning for more
Yelling for less
Yammering for branches
Between bordellos

The broken find me
Like black tangerines
Hanging from twisted tree

Teenagers on street corners
Of pumpkin orange

Knowing you
Is not possible
Without needing you

LA Skyline 13'

Where Did He Go?

6-26-14

Into the blank blank stare of beyond

The curdled mastery of space

The bed and breakfast of his skull

The unattached attachment of sky

He did not want to go
He was afraid to go

Yet he went in such grace and style

That even the great maker must have been surprised

In such faith for a man who questioned

In a democratic and fair manner

Into the licorice abyss
The tan nothingness

That even he my father must have known of something
In death that he never spoke of in life

Which Way?

8/23/15

Tossing and turning
Hiding and abiding

Perhaps the answer
Lies not in perfection
But in the attempt
At that there idealism

Not in bloody wolverine but
Hugging Nazarene

Bettering darkest nights
Not abandoning ugliest heights

Seeing the light in the sky
Not the bite in your eye or
The cry in the lie

First step counts the most
Next day mounts the ghost

Praying makes it so
Living takes away the crow

Radomir Vojtech Luza

Who I Am

Every moment is a battle
Against who I am

Against the nice boy
Who loves too easily
And gives too readily

The frightened child
Gazing into crevices for
The music he once heard

The forlorn traveler
Searching shadows for unknown criminals
Bathed in my blood

Each day a struggle against
The tide of mistakes that
Grow into triumphs

The prison cell of my mind
That once opened
Gathers the dust of ages
The crust of sages

But who am I?
Toiling against time
Tripping on a dime

Torn and tattered
Like a frustrated mime

Work to Do

Published in February, 2015 edition of online literary magazine KYSO Flash   12/10/14

Days blend like frozen Margaritas

One bending into another
None mattering
While mattering

Hours empty as carnival floats
Minutes missing memory
Seconds surprised

This life is a harmonica played in the dark
Trombone picked up in the afternoon
Acoustic guitar ambling towards egg white sky
Sinatra singing to slow surrender

And I hurt inside in black winter coat and dress shoes
Looking for the talent to live my life or
Just the faith to leave it alone

The momentum I had
Murdered by momentum

Working for the City

7/12/15

I want to work for the city
The Mecca I live in

I love cities
The way they smell
Sound and taste

The forgiven pleasure
I get from talking
To my neighbors

I want to run for the City Council
The body of government that
Makes it all happen

The law makers behind
Every rule and mule
In this town

I need to be in charge
Loom large
Like a construction barge

Not the state
Or some silly slate

We not me
Us not a selfish fuss
Maybe I'll just use a bus

Surround me with people and
A tall steeple and
And I will keep it simple

Writing

Embalming words on paper
On back cover of poetry notebook

Desperation thy name is verse
Shakespeare lives

Writing is letting go
Exercise of mind and heart

Poem flows through arm
From cranium to claw

Words feel authentic
Blood moves quickly

There is no money in poetry
People tell me

Unless you believe
From subject to soul
Syntax to syllable

That you are part of something larger
Genuinely changing the galaxy

Radomir Vojtech Luza

Wrongs of the Soul

Coming out of hiding
The soul stands on the corner of Perdition Street
With no friends to sell
No lover to accommodate

Unlock this cage
Release the choke hold on neutrality

Shine on
Shine bright

Out of my shell
Raging to hell
Love will abide
If taken in stride

Breathing is easy
Living is hard

Bring me the king
I will wrap him in string

It is not what we choose
But what chooses us

Yellow

11/23/14

Maybe the pain that followed the
Euphoria was worth it

Helping suffering turn to snow
Anger to wisdom
A stream into a waterfall

For what is art but experience
Divided by imagination
Passion multiplied by people
Juxtaposition juggling Jupiter

Perhaps the strain equaled the bane
Discipline suffusing the melancholic feign

I loved you once
When blue skies and turquoise
Rivers ruled the landscape of my heart

Now I am a pauper
Begging for pieces of time
Lost in moonglow and midnight

I am yellow

Born in Vienna, Austria in 1963, Radomir Vojtech Luza loves mixing voice with verse, syllables with solidarity and metaphors with meaning.

Luza gets his love of art and politics from his Czech parents, Radomir Sr. and Libuse Podhraska. The elder Luza fought in the Czech Resistance during WWII alongside his father, Vojtech, leader of the Czech Underground, who was murdered by the Nazis in 1944.

At 15, Podhraska was the youngest actress ever accepted into the Czech National Dramatic Conservatory where she loved studying the works of William Shakespeare and the early Greek playwrights before Adolf Hitler closed the doors in 1943.

The two then escaped Communism in their beloved Czechoslovakia in 1948 eventually coming to New York City in 1953 by way of Paris, France. In New York City, Luza Sr. received a PH.D in Eastern European history from New York University. He then taught Eastern European history at Tulane University in New Orleans for 25 years until he retired at the age of 70.

Podhraska died of ovarian cancer at the age of 72 in 2001 in Bucks County, PA outside of Philadelphia. Luza Sr. of lung failure in 2009 at an assisted living center in Montgomery County, PA in Philadelphia. He was 87.

The elder Luza now has an institute named after him at the University of New Orleans where he first started teaching. It is dedicated to the hours of painstaking research he did for the six scholarly books and numerous published articles he wrote. Luza Sr. was a trailblazer and ground breaker in the field of research.

But it is "The Hitler Kiss," Luza Sr.'s final book, which he penned with Christina Vella, that put him on the map as the subject of a tome and co-writer. The book, published by LSU press, describes the elder Luza's time in the Czech Resistance. Unlike any of his previous published work, the book is a personal and intimate thrill ride detailing a young man's experiences fighting for his beliefs and the father he loved from afar.

The younger Luza is the Poet Laureate of North Hollywood, CA, a Pushcart Prize nominee and the author of 25 books, 23 of which are collections of poetry.

Radomir has had his poetry published in nearly 70 literary journals, anthologies and websites such as "Poetic Diversity," "Askew," " KYSO Flash," "San Gabriel Valley Poetry Quarterly," "Bicycle Review," "Cultural Weekly," "Spare Change," "Nerve Cowboy," "Boston Globe," "Spectrum" and "Rogue Scholars.com," among others.

Luza 's poetry currently appears in four different anthologies at the same time: "Lummox IV," "Edgar Allan Poet's Journal #3," "The Altadena Poetry Review" and "Ne Se Hable Espanol."

Radomir, who graduated with a BA in English from Tulane University in New Orleans in 1985, has featured his poetry over 100 times across the country.

Luza, who also graduated from Jesuit High School in New Orleans in 1981, has hosted poetry series in cities such as New York City, Jersey City, NJ, Ft. Walton Beach, FLA and Los Angeles.

Radomir currently co-organizes and co-hosts the monthly UNBUCKLED: NoHo POETRY reading with Mary Anneeta Mann. At a little over five years, it is the longest running literary series in North Hollywood. The reading takes place on the First Saturday of each month from 3:45pm-5:45pm at T.U. Studios at 10943 Camarillo Street in North Hollywood, CA (Behind Odyssey Video) (Off Vineland) at the intersection of Camarillo, Vineland and Lankershim.

Radomir believes that poetry is the literary bridge to God.

And that God reads a little verse at breakfast, lunch and dinner.

Well, with the angels and Elvis.

To Luza, talent in poetry is defined by showing not telling, and from rich, textured imagery or verse that often come with the hard fought realizations that only art brings.

Printed in the United States
By Bookmasters